About This Book

Why This Book Is Important

Communication and Implementation: Sustaining the Practice, book six in the M&E series, discusses the importance of reporting results and sustaining the ROI Methodology within an organization. The worst situation is having program results and other data in hand and doing nothing with them. If the results are not communicated, decision makers will have no idea whether the programs have added value or whether the ROI Methodology is worth supporting.

Managers or others within an organization sometimes resist implementation of the ROI Methodology. To overcome resistance, concerns must be addressed, myths must be eliminated, and obstacles must be removed. This book examines the many ways in which these goals can be achieved.

What This Book Achieves

This book explains why and how to report ROI results and clarifies which audiences should be targeted for communication. It also explores ways to successfully implement the ROI process, gain support, and remove resistance.

How This Book Is Organized

This book describes how to report results and sustain the ROI Methodology. It begins with a brief introduction to the ROI process model and the Twelve Guiding Principles. Chapter One discusses why communication of ROI results is needed, the important principles of such communication, and how to plan the communication. How to develop the report and select the media for the report is detailed in this chapter as well. Finally, handling and analyzing the reactions to the communication are examined. Chapter Two explains how to implement the ROI Methodology; resistance to implementation must be mitigated, and the transition must be planned.

Chapter Three discusses the fundamental issues involved in gaining support for the ROI Methodology. The steps necessary to prepare the staff and remove obstacles are detailed. This chapter also covers how to select the programs for ROI evaluations, prepare the management team, and monitor progress. Chapter Four explores specific actions and best practices that can be used to ensure success with the ROI Methodology.

The Measurement and Evaluation Series

Editors

Patricia Pulliam Phillips, Ph.D.

Jack J. Phillips, Ph.D.

Introduction to the Measurement and Evaluation Series

The ROI Six Pack provides detailed information on developing ROI evaluations, implementing the ROI Methodology, and showing the value of a variety of functions and processes. With detailed examples, tools, templates, shortcuts, and checklists, this series will be a valuable reference for individuals interested in using the ROI Methodology to show the impact of their projects, programs, and processes.

The Need

Although financial ROI has been measured for over one hundred years to quantify the value of plants, equipment, and companies, the concept has only recently been applied to evaluate the impact of learning and development, human resources, technology, quality, marketing, and other support functions. In the learning and development field alone, the use of ROI has become routine in many organizations. In the past decade, hundreds of organizations have embraced the ROI process to show the impact of many different projects and programs.

Along the way, professionals and practitioners need help. They need tools, templates, and tips, along with explanations, examples, and details, to make this process work. Without this help, using the ROI Methodology to show the value of projects and programs is difficult. In short, practitioners need shortcuts and proven techniques to minimize the resources required to use this process. Practitioners' needs have created the need for this series. This series will provide the detail necessary to make the ROI Methodology successful within an organization. For easy reference and use, the books are logically arranged to align with the steps of the ROI Methodology.

Audience

The principal audience for these books is individuals who plan to use the ROI Methodology to show the value of their projects and programs. Such individuals are specialists or managers charged with proving the value of their particular project or program. They need detailed information, know-how, and confidence.

A second audience is those who have used the ROI Methodology for some time but want a quick reference with tips and techniques to make ROI implementation more successful within their organization. This series, which explains the evaluation process in detail, will be a valuable reference set for these individuals, regardless of other ROI publications owned.

A third audience is consultants and researchers who want to know how to address specific evaluation issues. Three important challenges face individuals as they measure ROI and conduct ROI evaluations: (1) collecting post-program data, (2) isolating the effects of the program, and (3) converting data to monetary values. A book is devoted to each of these critical issues, allowing researchers and consultants to easily find details on each issue.

A fourth audience is those who are curious about the ROI Methodology and its use. The first book in this series focuses specifically on ROI, its use, and how to determine whether it is appropriate for an organization. When interest is piqued, the remaining books provide more detail.

Flow of the Books

The six books are presented in a logical sequence, mirroring the ROI process model. Book one, *ROI Fundamentals: Why and When to Measure ROI*, presents the basic ROI Methodology and makes the business case for measuring ROI as it explores the benefits and barriers to implementation. It also examines the type of organization best suited for the ROI Methodology and the best time to implement it. Planning for an ROI evaluation is also explored in this book.

Book two, *Data Collection: Planning For and Collecting All Types of Data*, details data collection by examining the different techniques, methods, and issues involved in this process, with an emphasis on collecting post-program data. It examines the different data collection methods: questionnaires, interviews, focus groups, observation, action plans, performance contracts, and monitoring records.

Book three, *Isolation of Results: Defining the Impact of the Program*, focuses on the most valuable part of the ROI Methodology and the essential step for ensuring credibility. Recognizing that factors other than the program being measured can influence results, this book shows a variety of ways in which the effects of a program can be isolated from other influences. Techniques include comparison analysis using a control group, trend line analysis and forecasting methods, and expert input from a variety of sources.

Book four, *Data Conversion: Calculating the Monetary Benefits*, covers perhaps the second toughest challenge of ROI evaluation: placing monetary value on program benefits. To calculate the ROI, data must be converted to money, and *Data Conversion* shows how this conversion has been accomplished in a variety of organizations. The good news is that standard values are available for many items. When they are not, the book shows different techniques for converting them, ranging from calculating the value from records to seeking experts and searching databases. When data cannot be converted to money credibly and with minimum resources, they are considered intangible. This book explores the range of intangible benefits and the necessary techniques for collecting, analyzing, and recording them.

Book five, *Costs and ROI: Evaluating at the Ultimate Level,* focuses on costs and ROI. This book shows that all costs must be captured in order to create a fully loaded cost profile. All the costs must be included in order to be conservative and to give the analysis additional credibility. Next, the actual ROI calculation is presented, showing the various assumptions and issues that must be addressed when calculating the ROI. Three different calculations are presented: the benefit-cost ratio, the ROI percentage, and the payback period. The book concludes with several cautions and concerns about the use of ROI and its meaning.

Book six, *Communication and Implementation: Sustaining the Practice,* explores two important issues. The first issue is reporting the results of an evaluation. This is the final part of the ROI Methodology and is necessary to ensure that audiences have the information they need so that improvement processes can be implemented. A range of techniques is available, including face-to-face meetings, brief reports, one-page summaries, routine communications, mass-audience techniques, and electronic media. All are available for reporting evaluation results. The final part of the book focuses on how to sustain the ROI evaluation process: how to use it, keep it going, and make it work in the long term to add value to the organization and, often, to show the value of all the programs and projects within a function or department.

Terminology: Programs, Projects, Solutions

In this series the terms *program* and *project* are used to describe many processes that can be evaluated using the ROI Methodology. This is an important issue because readers may vary widely in their perspectives. Individuals involved in technology applications may

Table I.1. Terms and Applications

Term	Example
Program	Leadership development skills enhancement for senior executives
Project	A reengineering scheme for a plastics division
System	A fully interconnected network for all branches of a bank
Initiative	A faith-based effort to reduce recidivism
Policy	A new preschool plan for disadvantaged citizens
Procedure	A new scheduling arrangement for truck drivers
Event	A golf outing for customers
Meeting	A U.S. Coast Guard conference on innovations
Process	Quality sampling
People	Staff additions in the customer care center
Tool	A new means of selecting hotel staff

use the terms *system* and *technology* rather than *program* or *project*. In public policy, in contrast, the word *program* is prominent. For a professional meetings and events planner, the word *program* may not be pertinent, but in human resources, *program* is often used. Finding one term for all these situations would be difficult. Consequently, the terms *program* and *project* are used interchangeably. Table I.1 lists these and other terms that may be used in other contexts.

Features

Each book in the series takes a straightforward approach to make it understandable, practical, and useful. Checklists are provided, charts are included, templates are presented, and examples are explored. All are intended to show how the ROI Methodology works. The focus of these books is implementing the process and making it successful within an organization. The methodology is based on the work of hundreds of individuals who have made the ROI Methodology a successful evaluation process within their organizations.

About Pfeiffer

Pfeiffer serves the professional development and hands-on resource needs of training and human resource practitioners and gives them products to do their jobs better. We deliver proven ideas and solutions from experts in HR development and HR management, and we offer effective and customizable tools to improve workplace performance. From novice to seasoned professional, Pfeiffer is the source you can trust to make yourself and your organization more successful.

Essential Knowledge Pfeiffer produces insightful, practical, and comprehensive materials on topics that matter the most to training and HR professionals. Our Essential Knowledge resources translate the expertise of seasoned professionals into practical, how-to guidance on critical workplace issues and problems. These resources are supported by case studies, worksheets, and job aids and are frequently supplemented with CD-ROMs, websites, and other means of making the content easier to read, understand, and use.

Essential Tools Pfeiffer's Essential Tools resources save time and expense by offering proven, ready-to-use materials—including exercises, activities, games, instruments, and assessments—for use during a training or team-learning event. These resources are frequently offered in looseleaf or CD-ROM format to facilitate copying and customization of the material.

Pfeiffer also recognizes the remarkable power of new technologies in expanding the reach and effectiveness of training. While e-hype has often created whizbang solutions in search of a problem, we are dedicated to bringing convenience and enhancements to proven training solutions. All our e-tools comply with rigorous functionality standards. The most appropriate technology wrapped around essential content yields the perfect solution for today's on-the-go trainers and human resource professionals.

Pfeiffer *Essential resources for training and HR professionals*
www.pfeiffer.com

Communication and Implementation

Sustaining the Practice

Jack J. Phillips, Ph.D.
Wendi Friedman Tush, M.B.A.

Pfeiffer
A Wiley Imprint
www.pfeiffer.com

Published by Pfeiffer
An Imprint of Wiley
989 Market Street, San Francisco, CA 94103-1741
www.pfeiffer.com

For additional copies/bulk purchases of this book in the U.S. please contact 800-274-4434.

Pfeiffer books and products are available through most bookstores. To contact Pfeiffer directly call our Customer Care Department within the U.S. at 800-274-4434, outside the U.S. at 317-572-3985, fax 317-572-4002, or visit www.pfeiffer.com.

Pfeiffer also publishes its books in a variety of electronic formats. Some content that appears in print may not be available in electronic books.

Library of Congress Cataloging-in-Publication Data

Phillips, Jack J., date.
   Communication and implementation: sustaining the practice/Jack J. Phillips, Wendi Friedman Tush.
      p. cm.
   Includes bibliographical references and index.
   ISBN: 978-0-7879-8722-0 (pbk.)
   1. Communication in personnel management.   2. Employees—Training of.
3. Communication in management. I. Tush, Wendi Friedman, date. II. Title.
   HF5549.5.C6P53 2008
   658.3—dc22

                                                                    2007046924

Production Editor: Michael Kay   Editorial Assistant: Julie Rodriguez
Editor: Matthew Davis   Manufacturing Supervisor: Becky Morgan

Printed in the United States of America

PB Printing 10 9 8 7 6 5 4 3 2 1

Contents

Chapter 4: Sustaining the Use of the ROI Methodology: Keeping the Process on Track   129

Acknowledgments from the Editors

From Patti

No project, regardless of its size or scope, is completed without the help and support of others. My sincere thanks go to the staff at Pfeiffer. Their support for this project has been relentless. Matt Davis has been the greatest! It is our pleasure and privilege to work with such a professional and creative group of people.

Thanks also go to my husband, Jack. His unwavering support of my work is always evident. His idea for the series was to provide readers with a practical understanding of the various components of a comprehensive measurement and evaluation process. Thank you, Jack, for another fun opportunity!

From Jack

Many thanks go to the staff who helped make this series a reality. Lori Ditoro did an excellent job of meeting a very tight deadline and delivering a quality manuscript.

Much admiration and thanks go to Patti. She is an astute observer of the ROI Methodology, having observed and learned from hundreds of presentations, consulting assignments, and engagements. In addition, she is an excellent researcher and student of the process, studying how it is developed and how it works. She has become an ROI expert in her own right. Thanks, Patti, for your many contributions. You are a great partner, friend, and spouse.

Principles of the ROI Methodology

The ROI Methodology is a step-by-step tool for evaluating any program, project, or initiative in any organization. Figure P.1 illustrates the ROI process model, which makes a potentially complicated process simple by breaking it into sequential steps. The ROI process model provides a systematic, step-by-step approach to ROI evaluations that helps keep the process manageable, allowing users to address one issue at a time. The model also emphasizes that the ROI Methodology is a logical, systematic process that flows from one step to another and provides a way for evaluators to collect and analyze six types of data.

Applying the model consistently from one program to another is essential for successful evaluation. To aid consistent application of the model, the ROI Methodology is based on twelve Guiding Principles. These principles are necessary for a credible, conservative approach to evaluation through the different levels.

1. When conducting a higher-level evaluation, collect data at lower levels.
2. When planning a higher-level evaluation, the previous level of evaluation is not required to be comprehensive.
3. When collecting and analyzing data, use only the most credible sources.

Figure P.1. The ROI Process Model

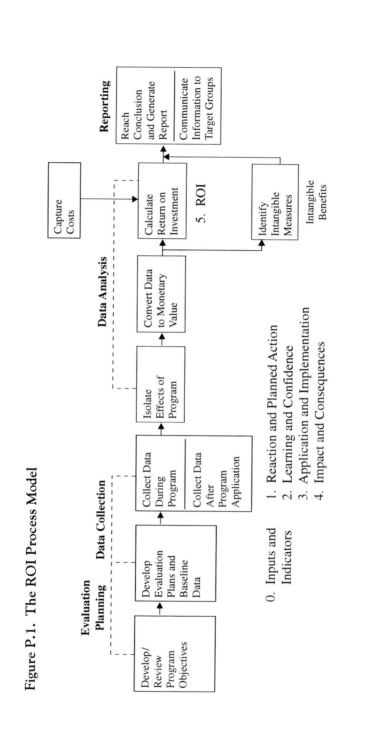

Evaluation Planning

Data Collection

Data Analysis

Reporting

Develop/ Review Program Objectives

Develop Evaluation Plans and Baseline Data

Collect Data During Program

Collect Data After Program Application

Isolate Effects of Program

Convert Data to Monetary Value

Calculate Return on Investment

5. ROI

Capture Costs

Identify Intangible Measures

Intangible Benefits

Reach Conclusion and Generate Report

Communicate Information to Target Groups

0. Inputs and Indicators

1. Reaction and Planned Action
2. Learning and Confidence
3. Application and Implementation
4. Impact and Consequences

4. When analyzing data, select the most conservative alternative for calculations.

5. Use at least one method to isolate the effects of a project.

6. If no improvement data are available for a population or from a specific source, assume that little or no improvement has occurred.

7. Adjust estimates of improvement for potential errors of estimation.

8. Avoid use of extreme data items and unsupported claims when calculating ROI.

9. Use only the first year of annual benefits in ROI analysis of short-term solutions.

10. Fully load all costs of a solution, project, or program when analyzing ROI.

11. Intangible measures are defined as measures that are purposely not converted to monetary values.

12. Communicate the results of the ROI Methodology to all key stakeholders.

1

Reporting Results

O nce the data collection and the ROI analysis are completed, the real fun begins. All the results need to be organized into a report and communicated to appropriate parties. Preparing for this final stage of the ROI process requires some thought on the following questions. Should the data be used to modify the program, change the process, show the contribution, justify new programs, gain additional support, or build goodwill? How should the data be presented, and who should present them? Where should the presentation take place? Who should hear the presentation, and who should receive a report? These and other questions are examined in this chapter. The worst course of action is to do nothing with the data. Communicating the results is as important as achieving them. This chapter explains how to present evaluation data to different audiences in both oral and written formats.

The Importance of Communication

Communicating results is a critical issue in the ROI Methodology. While it is important to communicate results to interested stakeholders after a program is complete, communication throughout the program is important as well. A regular flow of information ensures that necessary adjustments can be made and that all stakeholders are aware of the successes and issues of the program. There are at least five key reasons to be concerned about communicating results:

1. *Measurement and evaluation mean nothing without communication.* Measuring success and collecting evaluation data mean nothing unless the findings are promptly communicated to the appropriate audiences, making them aware of what is occurring and allowing them to take action if necessary. Communication is necessary so that program results can be put to use quickly and aggressively.

2. *Communication is necessary in order to make improvements.* Information is collected at different points during the program process. This allows adjustments to be made to the process along the way; however, this can happen only when the information is communicated to the appropriate audience. Therefore, the quality and timeliness of communication become critical issues when adjustments or improvements are required. Even after a program is completed, communication is necessary to make sure that the target audience fully understands the results and how the results could be used to enhance current or future programs. Communication is the key to making important adjustments at all phases of a program.

3. *Communication is needed in order to explain the contributions of a program.* Explaining the contribution of a program by means of six major types of measures can be complex. Target audiences need a thorough explanation of the results—especially business impact and ROI. The quality of a well-executed communication strategy—including the techniques, the media, and the overall process used—will determine the extent to which the audiences understand the contribution of a program. Communication must be planned and implemented with the goal of ensuring that the audiences understand the full impact of the program.

4. *Communication can be a sensitive issue.* Communication is a critical function that can cause major problems if it is mishandled. Especially when the results of a program are closely linked to the performance of others or to political issues within an organization, the communication may upset some individuals and please others. If certain individuals do not receive the information or if it is delivered inconsistently from one group to another, problems may quickly surface. It is important that the communication is properly constructed and effectively delivered to all the individuals who need the information.

5. *Different audiences need different information.* Communication must be tailored directly to the needs of different stakeholders. Planning and effort must be employed to make sure that each audience receives all the information it needs, in the proper format and at the proper time. A single report for all audiences may not be appropriate. The scope and size of the report, the media used, and even the types and levels of information included will vary significantly from one group to another. In other words, the makeup of the target audience determines which communication process is appropriate.

The preceding reasons indicate why communication is a critical issue, although its role in a program is often overlooked or underestimated. This chapter further explores this important issue and provides a variety of techniques for effective communication to any target audience.

Principles of Communicating Results

The skills required to successfully communicate program results are almost as intricate and sophisticated as those needed to obtain the results. The style is as important as the substance. Regardless of the message, audience, or medium, a few general principles apply. These general principles are important to the overall success of the communication effort and should be used as a checklist for the program team as it disseminates program results.

Timely Communication

As a rule, results should be communicated as soon as they are known. From a practical standpoint, it may be best to delay the communication until a convenient time, such as the next general management meeting or publication of the next newsletter. The timing of the communication should be consciously addressed. Is the audience ready for the results in light of other things that have happened or are currently happening? Does the audience expect the results? When is the best time to communicate in order to achieve the maximum effect on the audience? Do circumstances dictate a change in the timing of the communication?

Targeted Communication

Communication will be more effective if it is designed for a particular group. The message should be specifically tailored to the interests, needs, and expectations of the target audience.

The program results described in this chapter reflect outcomes at all levels, including the six types of data discussed in this series. Some of the data are collected early in a program and are communicated during the program. Other data are collected after implementation and communicated in a follow-up study. Thus, the program results range from early feedback in qualitative terms to ROI values in varying degrees of quantitative terms. Choices should be made up front about who needs to see the results and in how much detail.

Effective Media Selection

For particular groups, some media may be more effective than others. Face-to-face meetings may be better than special bulletins. A memo distributed exclusively to top management may be more effective than the company newsletter. The proper method of communication can help improve the effectiveness of the process.

Unbiased Communication

It is important to make sure that the communication is accurate, credible, and objective, both in fact and in appearance. Some audiences view these results with great skepticism, anticipating biased opinions. Boastful statements may turn off recipients, and as a result, most of the content is lost on them. Observable, believable facts carry far more weight than extreme or sensational claims. Although such claims may get the audience's attention, they often detract from the credibility of the results.

Consistent Communication

The timing and content of the communication should be consistent with past practices. A special communication at an unusual time may provoke suspicion. Also, if a particular group, such as top management, regularly receives communication on outcomes, it should continue receiving that communication—even if the results are not positive. If some results are omitted, it will leave the impression that only positive results are being reported.

Testimonials from Respected Individuals

Individuals' opinions are strongly influenced by other people, particularly those who are respected and trusted. Testimonials about program results from individuals who are respected by others in the organization (particularly the target audience for the communication) can positively influence the effectiveness of the message. The credibility of the individual may be related to his or her leadership ability, position, special skills, or knowledge. In contrast, a testimonial from an individual who commands little respect and has little credibility may have a negative impact on the message.

Communication Strategy Shaped by the Audience's Opinion of the Program Team

Opinions are difficult to change, and a pre-existing negative opinion of the program team may not change with a simple presentation of facts. However, communicating the facts may help strengthen the opinions held by existing supporters. It helps reinforce their position and provides a defense when they discuss the program with others. A team with a high level of credibility and respect may have an easy time communicating results. Low credibility can create problems when trying to be persuasive. Thus, the reputation of the program team should be a consideration when the overall communication strategy is being developed.

Analysis of the Need for Communication

The specific reasons for communicating program results depend on the program, the setting, and the unique needs of the sponsor. Following are the most common reasons:

- *To secure approval for a program and allocation of time and money.* The initial communication about a program presents a proposal, a projected ROI, or other data that are intended to secure approval for the program. This communication may not have much data but anticipates the data to come.

- *To gain support for a program and its objectives.* Support from a variety of groups within an organization is important to the success of a program. Often, communication is intended to build this support to allow a program to work successfully.

- *To secure agreement on issues, solutions, and resources.* As a program begins, all who are directly involved must agree on and understand the important elements and requirements of the program.

- *To build the credibility of a program or a program team.* Early in the process of developing a program, the audience should understand the approach and reputation of the program team, the techniques that it will use, and its expected products. The audience should understand the commitments that must be made by all parties as a result of the approach that has been chosen.

- *To reinforce program processes.* Key managers must support a program and reinforce the processes used in its design, development, and delivery. Some communication is designed to facilitate those processes.

- *To drive action for program improvements.* Sometimes, communication early in the process of creating a program is designed as a process improvement tool, in order to effect changes and improvements as needs are uncovered and as individuals make suggestions.

- *To prepare participants for a program.* Those most directly involved in a program, the participants, must be prepared for the learning, the application of that learning, and the responsibilities that will be required of them in order to make the program a success.

- *To improve results and obtain quality feedback in the future.* Some communication is designed to update stakeholders on the status of a program and to influence decisions, seek support, or communicate events and expectations to key stakeholders. In addition, it will enhance both the quality and quantity of information provided in the future as stakeholders see the feedback cycle in action.

- *To show the complete results of a program.* The most important communication of the program cycle occurs after data on the results of a program have been collected and analyzed. At this time, the results from all six types of measures are communicated to the appropriate individuals so that they have a full understanding of the success or shortcomings of the program.

- *To underscore the importance of measuring results.* Some individuals need to understand or be convinced of the importance of measurement and evaluation. They must be made to see the need for having important data on the measures that matter to the organization.

- *To explain the techniques used to measure results.* The program sponsor and support staff need to understand the techniques used in measuring the results; they need to know that a sound theoretical framework has been used. In some cases, the techniques may be transferred internally and used to measure the results of other programs.

- *To stimulate participants to become involved in a program.* Ideally, participants will want to be involved in the program that is being offered. Communication is designed to pique their interest in the program and inform them of its importance.

- *To stimulate interest in the department or function that produced a program.* Some communications are designed to create interest in all the products and services offered by a unit or department, based on the results of current programs.

- *To demonstrate accountability for expenditures.* All individuals involved must understand the need for accountability and the approach that the program team uses to address that need. Communicating these points helps to ensure accountability for program expenditures.

- *To market future programs.* Building a database of successful programs is important. Past successes can be used to convince others that programs can add value.

Although the preceding list is quite comprehensive, there may be other reasons for communicating program results. The specifics of each situation should be considered when the program team is developing reports to communicate program results.

Communication Planning

Planning is also a critical part of communicating the results of major programs. Planning the communication is important in order to ensure that each audience receives the proper information at the right time and that appropriate actions are taken. Three elements are important in planning the communication of program results: general communication policies, the communication plan for the entire program, and the communication plan for the impact study.

Communication Policies

Some general policies need to be developed when planning the communication of program results. Seven questions require attention as the policies are developed.

1. *What will be communicated?* The types of information that will be communicated should be detailed. The six types of data from the ROI model should be included, and the overall progress of the program should be described.
2. *When will the data be communicated?* In all communication, timing is critical. If adjustments need to be made to the program,

the information should be communicated quickly so that swift action can be taken.

3. *How will the information be communicated?* Different audiences and different organizations prefer different communication media. For example, some managers prefer written reports, others prefer face-to-face meetings, and still others want their employees to use electronic communications whenever possible.

4. *Where will the communication take place?* Some stakeholder groups prefer that communication take place close to the program sponsor; others prefer the central offices. The location can be an important issue in terms of convenience and perception.

5. *Who will communicate the information?* Will the program team, an independent consultant, or an individual from the sponsor's office communicate the information? The person communicating must have credibility so that the information will be believed and accepted.

6. *Who is the target audience?* Target audiences that should always receive information should be identified as well as others who will receive information when appropriate.

7. *What specific actions are required or desired?* In some cases, when information is presented no action is needed. In other situations, changes are desired and sometimes required.

These seven issues should frame the policy that governs communication as a whole.

Communication Plan for the Entire Program

The communication plan for a major program is usually developed when the program is approved. This plan details how specific information will be developed and communicated to various groups, and it identifies the expected actions that will be taken on the basis of the information. In addition, the plan details how the overall results will be communicated, the time frames for communication, and the appropriate groups to receive the information. The program team and the sponsor need to agree on the extent of the detail required in the communication plan. Additional information on communication planning for an entire program is provided later in this chapter.

Communication Plan for the Impact Study

A third element in communicating program results is the plan to present the results of the specific impact study. This communication occurs when a major program is completed and the detailed results are known. Two important issues to address are who should receive the results and in what form. The communication plan for the final impact study is more specialized than the plan for the entire program. Table 1.1 shows the communication plan for the impact study of a major stress reduction program. Teams had been experiencing high levels of stress; through numerous activities and behavior changes brought about by the program, stress began to diminish among the teams.

In this case, five communication pieces were developed, each for a different audience. The complete seventy-five-page report on the ROI impact study, which served as the historical document for the program, went to the sponsor, the program team, and the manager of each of the participant teams involved in the studies. The executive summary, a much smaller document, went to high-level executives. A general interest overview and summary, without the ROI calculation, went to the participants. A general interest article was developed for company publications, and a brochure was developed to highlight the success of the program. The brochure was used to market the same program internally to other teams and served as additional marketing material for the program team. The detailed communication plan for the impact study may be

Table 1.1. Communication Plan for the Impact of a Major Program

Communication Document	Communication Targets	Distribution Method
Complete report with appendixes (75 pages)	• Program sponsor • Program team • Participants' managers	Distribute and discuss in a special meeting
Executive summary (8 pages)	• Senior management in the business units • Senior corporate management	Distribute and discuss in a routine meeting
General interest overview and summary without the ROI calculation (10 pages)	• Participants	Mail with a letter
General interest article (1 page)	• All employees	Publish in a company publication
Brochure highlighting the program, objectives, and specific results	• Team leaders with an interest in the program • Prospective sponsors of future programs	Include with other marketing materials

part of the overall communication plan for the project but may be fine-tuned as the impact study develops.

———————

These plans underscore the importance of organizing the communication strategy for a program.

Audience Selection

Not everyone in an organization needs to see or hear the results of a program. Early in the process, the audiences should be chosen and a decision made about how much information each group should receive. This section details the selection process and the criteria for selecting each audience.

Preliminary Issues

When considering an audience, ask the following questions about the members of each group:

- Are they interested in the program?

- Do they want to receive the information?

- Has someone already made a commitment to them about receiving the communication?

- Is the timing right for communicating with this audience?

- Are they familiar with the program?

- How would they prefer to receive the results?

- Do they know the program team members?

- Are they likely to find the results threatening?

- Which medium will be most convincing to this group?

For each potential target audience, three actions are needed:

1. To the greatest extent possible, the program team should know and understand the target audience.

2. The program team should find out what information is needed and why. Each group will have its own needs in relation to the information desired. Some will want detailed information, while others will want brief information. Input from others should be used to help determine what the audience needs and wants.

3. The program team should try to understand audience biases. Some audiences will tend toward a particular bias or opinion, while other audiences will represent a variety of different opinions. Some will quickly support the results, whereas others may be against them or be neutral. The staff should be empathetic and try to understand differing views. With this understanding, communications can be tailored to each group. Understanding the biases of an audience is especially critical when an audience may react negatively to the results.

Basis for Selecting the Audience

The audiences targeted to receive information on results are likely to be varied in terms of job levels and responsibilities. Determining which groups will receive a particular communication piece deserves careful thought, for problems can arise when a group receives inappropriate information or when a group is omitted altogether. A sound basis for audience selection is analysis of the reason for the communication. Table 1.2 shows common target audiences and the basis for selecting them.

Perhaps the most important audience is the sponsor—the individual or team supporting the ROI study. This individual (or group) initiates the program, reviews data, and weighs the final assessment of the effectiveness of the program.

Table 1.2. Common Target Audiences for Communication of Program Results

Reason for Communication	Target Audiences
To secure approval for a program	Sponsor, top executives
To gain support for a program	Immediate managers, team leaders
To secure agreement on the issues	Participants, team leaders
To build the credibility of a program	Top executives
To reinforce program processes	Immediate managers
To drive action for improvement	Sponsor, program team
To prepare participants for a program	Team leaders
To improve results and the quality of future feedback	Participants
To show the complete results of a program	Sponsor
To underscore the importance of measuring results	Sponsor, program team
To explain the techniques used to measure results	Sponsor, support staff
To stimulate participant involvement	Participants' team leaders
To stimulate interest in the functional unit that produced a program	Top executives
To demonstrate accountability for expenditures	All employees
To market future programs	Prospective sponsors

Another important target audience is the senior management group. This group is responsible for allocating resources to the program and needs information to help justify expenditures and gauge the effectiveness of the efforts.

Selected groups of managers (or all managers) are also important target audiences. Management's support and involvement in the process and the department's credibility are important to success. Effectively communicating program results to management can increase both support and credibility.

Communicating with the participants' team leaders or immediate managers is essential. In many cases, they must encourage the participants to implement the program. Also, they often support and reinforce the objectives of the program.

Occasionally, results are communicated in order to encourage participation in a program, especially if participation is voluntary. In such cases, potential participants are important targets for communication.

Participants need feedback on the overall success of the program effort. Some individuals may not have been as successful as others in achieving the desired results. Communicating the results puts additional pressure on participants to effectively implement the program and improve future results. For those who are already achieving excellent results, the communication will serve as a reinforcement of the program. Communicating results to participants is often overlooked; it is sometimes assumed that once the program is complete, there is no point in informing them of its success.

The program team must receive information about program results. Those who have designed, developed, facilitated, or implemented a program must be given information on its effectiveness, whether it is a small program on which the program team receives a brief update or a large program on which a complete program team needs detailed feedback. Evaluation information is necessary so that adjustments can be made if a program is not as effective as it could be.

An organization's support staff should receive detailed information about the measurement and evaluation process. This group provides support services to the program team, usually as part of the same department.

Company employees and stockholders may be less likely targets. General interest news stories may increase employee respect for a program. Goodwill and positive attitudes toward an organization may also be by-products of communicating program results. Stockholders, on the other hand, are more interested in the return on their investment.

While Table 1.2 shows the most common target audiences, there may be others within an organization. For instance, management or employees could be subdivided into different departments, divisions, or even subsidiaries of the organization that may have different reasons to be interested in program results. In a complex organization, the number of audiences can be large. At a minimum, we recommend that program results be communicated to four target audiences: the senior management group, the participants' immediate manager or team leader, the participants, and the program team.

Development of the Information: The Impact Study

The decision on the type of formal evaluation report to be prepared will depend on how much detail should be presented to the target audiences. Brief summaries of results with appropriate charts may be sufficient for some communication efforts. In other situations, particularly when significant programs with extensive funding are involved, the amount of detail in the evaluation report is more crucial. A complete and comprehensive report on the impact study may be necessary. This report can then be abridged and tailored for specific audiences and for different media. The full impact study should include the major components discussed in this section.

Executive Summary

The executive summary is a brief overview of the entire report, explaining the basis for the evaluation and the significant conclusions and recommendations. It is designed for individuals who are too busy to read a detailed report. It is usually written last but appears first in the report for easy access.

Background Information

The background information provides a general description of the program. If applicable, the needs assessment that led to implementation of the program is summarized. The program is fully described, including the events that led to the intervention. Other specific items necessary to provide a full description of the program are included. The extent of detailed information depends on the amount of information that the audience needs.

Objectives

The objectives for both the impact study and the program are outlined. Sometimes, they are the same, but they may be different. The report details the objectives of the study itself so that the reader can clearly understand the rationale for the study and how the data will be used. In addition, specific program objectives are detailed because they form the basis for collecting the different levels of data.

Evaluation Strategy or Methodology

The evaluation strategy outlines all the components that make up the total evaluation process. The specific purposes of evaluation are outlined, and the evaluation design and methodology are explained. The instruments used in data collection are described and presented as exhibits. Any unusual issues or other useful information related to the design, timing, and execution of the evaluation are also included.

Data Collection and Analysis

This section explains the methods used to collect the data. Such methods were detailed in *Data Collection*, book two of this series. The data collected are usually summarized in the report, and then the methods used to analyze the data are presented, along with any interpretations that have been made. Among other issues covered, isolation and data conversion techniques are presented in this section.

Program Costs

Program costs are presented in this section of the report. A summary of the costs, by category, is included. For example, analysis, development, implementation, and evaluation costs are recommended categories for cost presentation. The assumptions made in developing and classifying the costs are also discussed in this section.

Reaction and Planned Action

This section details the data collected from key stakeholders, particularly the participants of the program, to measure their reaction to the program and to determine what actions they planned to take following the program. Other input from the sponsor or managers may be included in order to show their reactions and their satisfaction with the program.

Learning and Confidence

This section contains a brief summary of the formal and informal methods that were used to measure learning. The results of those measurements explain how participants have learned the new processes, skills, tasks, procedures, and practices presented in the program and describe participants' confidence in their ability to use or apply this new knowledge.

Application and Implementation

This section details how the program was implemented and the success that the participants experienced in applying their new skills and knowledge. Implementation issues are addressed, including any major success or lack of success.

Business Impact

This section explains the business impact measures that were used, which represent the business needs that initially drove the program. The data from these measures show the extent to which performance changed during implementation of the program.

Return on Investment

This section shows the ROI calculation, along with the benefit-cost ratio. It compares the value to what was expected and provides an interpretation of the calculation.

Intangible Measures

This section describes the intangible measures that are directly linked to the program. Intangible measures are measures that are not converted to monetary values or included in the ROI calculation.

Barriers and Enablers

Barriers to implementation—the problems and obstacles that affect the success of the program—are detailed. In addition, enablers—factors or influences that positively affect the program—are described. Barriers and enablers provide insight into what might hinder or enhance programs in the future.

Conclusions and Recommendations

This section presents conclusions based on all the results. If appropriate, brief explanations of how each conclusion was reached are presented. A list of recommendations or changes in the program, if appropriate, is provided, along with brief explanations of each recommendation. The conclusions and recommendations must be consistent with one another and with the findings described in the previous sections of the report.

Report Development

Exhibit 1.1 shows the table of contents of a typical report on an ROI evaluation. This format represents an effective, professional way to present ROI data.

Potential trouble spots need to be observed. This document reports on the success of a group of employees; therefore, credit for the success must actually be given to the participants and their immediate managers. Their performance generated the success, and that should be made clear in the report.

Another important caution: avoid boasting about the results. Although the ROI Methodology may be an accurate and credible process, it still has some subjective issues. Huge claims of success may quickly turn off an audience and interfere with the delivery of the desired message.

A final issue concerns the structure of the report. The methodology should be clearly explained, along with any assumptions made in the analysis. The reader should be able to readily see how the values were developed and how specific steps were followed to make the process more conservative, credible, and accurate. Detailed statistical analyses should be placed in the appendixes.

Selection of Communication Media

Many options are available to communicate program results. In addition to the impact study report and macro-level scorecard (discussed later in this chapter), the most frequently used media are meetings, interim and progress reports, the organization's publications, e-mail, brochures, and case studies. Exhibit 1.2 provides a summary of the various media used to communicate results.

Meetings

Meetings are fertile ground for communicating program results. All organizations have meetings. But it is important to choose the

Exhibit 1.1. Format of an Impact Study Report

I.   Executive Summary

II.   General Information
- Background
- Objectives of the Study

III. Methodology for the Impact Study
- Evaluation Framework
- The ROI Methodology
- Data Collection Strategy
- ROI Analysis Strategy
  - Isolating the Effects of the Program
  - Converting Data to Monetary Values
  - Program Costs

This section builds credibility for the process.

IV.   Results: General Information
- Response Profile
- Success with Objectives

V.   Results: Reaction and Planned
- Data Sources
- Data Summary
- Key Issues

VI.   Results: Learning and Confidence
- Data Sources
- Data Summary
- Key Issues

VII. Results: Application and Implementation
- Data Sources
- Data Summary
- Barriers to Application
- Enablers of Application
- Key Issues

The results from six measures: Levels 1, 2, 3, 4, 5, and intangibles tell the complete story of program success.

VIII. Results: Business Impact
- General Comments
- Linkage with Business Measures
- Key Issues

IX.   Results: ROI and Its Meaning

X.   Results: Intangible Measures

XI.   Conclusions and Recommendations
- Conclusions
- Recommendations

XII. Appendixes

Exhibit 1.2. Options for Communicating Program Results

Meetings	Detailed Reports	Brief Reports	Electronic Reporting	Mass Publications
Executives	Impact study	Executive summary	Web site	Announcements
Managers	Case study (internal)	Slide overview	E-mail	Bulletins
Stakeholders	Case study (external)	One-page summary	Blog	Newsletters
Staff	Major articles	Brochure	Video	Brief articles

proper context for reporting results. A few examples illustrate the variety of meetings, including some that are listed in Exhibit 1.2, and indicate how program results can be worked into the format of each.

Staff Meetings

Throughout the chain of command, staff meetings are held to review progress, discuss current problems, and distribute information. These meetings can be an excellent forum for discussing the results achieved in a major program when it relates to the group's activities. Program results can be sent to executives for use in staff meetings, or a member of the program team can attend the meeting to make the presentation.

Manager Meetings

Regular meetings of frontline managers are quite common. Typically, ways to help their work units are discussed. Thus, discussion of a program and its results can be integrated into the regular meeting format.

Best-Practice Meetings

Some organizations have best-practice meetings or videoconferences in order to discuss recent successes and best practices. These present excellent opportunities to learn about methodologies (such as those addressed in programs) and to share results.

Business Update Meetings

Some organizations hold a periodic meeting for all members of management in which the CEO reviews progress and discusses plans for the coming year. A few highlights of major program results can be integrated into the CEO's speech, indicating top executive interest, commitment, and support. Results are mentioned along with operating profit, new facilities and equipment, new company acquisitions, and the coming year's sales forecast.

Progress Reports

A highly visible way to communicate results is through routine memos and progress reports. This method is usually used only for large programs. Published or disseminated via the intranet on a periodic basis, they usually have several purposes:

- To inform management about the status of a program

- To communicate periodic results achieved in a program

- To activate needed changes and improvements

A more subtle reason for progress reports may be to gain additional support and commitment from the management group and thus keep a program intact. Progress reports are produced by the program team and distributed to a select group of managers in the organization. Format and scope vary considerably. Common topics include the following:

- *Schedule of activities*. A schedule of planned steps or activities should be an integral part of this report. A brief description of the activities should also be presented.

- *Reactions from participants*. A brief summary of reaction evaluations in order to report initial success may be appropriate. Also, brief interviews with participants might be included.

- *Results*. A key focus of a progress report is the results achieved from the program. Significant results that can be documented should be presented in an easy-to-understand format. The method (or methods) of evaluation should be briefly outlined, along with the measurement data.

- *Changes in responsibilities*. Occasionally, people involved in planning, developing, implementing, or evaluating a program are reassigned, transferred, or promoted. How these changes affect responsibilities and the program must be communicated.

- *Participant spotlight*. A section that highlights a participant can focus additional attention on results. This section provides an opportunity to recognize outstanding participants who are responsible for excellent results and bring attention to unusual achievements.

While the items on the preceding list may not be suitable for every report, they represent topics that should be presented to the management group. When produced in a professional manner, progress reports can improve management support and commitment to the effort.

Organizational Publications and Standard Communication Tools

To reach a wide audience, the program team can use in-house publications. Whether a newsletter, magazine, newspaper, or electronic file, these media usually reach all employees. The information can be quite effective if communicated appropriately. The scope should be limited to general interest articles, announcements, and interviews. Following are the types of issues that should be covered in these publications.

- *Program results.* Results communicated through these media must be significant enough to arouse general interest. For example, a story with the headline "Safety Training Program Helps Produce One Million Hours Without a Lost-Time Accident" will catch the attention of many people because they may have participated in the program and can appreciate the significance of the results. Reports on the accomplishments of a small group of participants may not create interest unless the audience can relate to the accomplishments.

For many program implementations, results are achieved weeks or even months after the program is completed. Participants need reinforcement from many sources. If results are communicated to a general audience, including a participant's subordinates or peers, additional pressure to continue with the program or similar ones in the future occurs.

- *Participant recognition.* General audience communication can bring recognition to participants, particularly those who excel in some aspect of a program. When participants deliver unusual performance, public recognition can enhance their self-esteem.

- *Human interest stories.* Many human interest stories can come out of major programs. A rigorous program with

difficult requirements can provide the basis for an
interesting story on participants who implement the
program. In one organization, the editor of the company
newsletter participated in a demanding program and
wrote a stimulating article about what being a participant was like. The article gave the reader a tour of the
entire program and its effectiveness in terms of the
results achieved. It was an interesting and effective way
to provide information about a challenging
activity.

The benefits are many and the opportunities endless for a program team to use in-house publications and company-wide intranets to let others know about successful programs.

E-Mail and Electronic Media

Internal and external Web pages on the Internet, company-wide
intranets, and e-mail are excellent vehicles for releasing results,
promoting ideas, and informing employees and other target groups
about results. E-mail, in particular, provides a virtually instanta-
neous method of communicating with and soliciting responses from
large numbers of people.

Brochures

A brochure might be appropriate for programs that are conducted
on a continuing basis and in which participants have produced excellent results. A brochure should be attractive and should present
a complete description of a program, with a major section devoted
to results obtained by previous participants, if available. Measur-
able results, reactions from participants, or direct quotes from other
individuals can add spice.

Case Studies

Case studies are an effective way to communicate the results of a program; thus, it may be useful to develop a few program evaluations in a case study format. A typical case study provides background information (including the situation or events that led to the intervention), presents the techniques and strategies used to develop the study, and highlights the key issues in the program. Case studies tell an interesting story of how an evaluation was developed and the problems and concerns identified along the way.

Case studies have many additional useful applications within an organization. First, they can be used in group discussions, during which interested individuals can react to the material, offer different perspectives, and draw conclusions about approaches or techniques. Second, the case study can serve as a self-teaching guide for individuals who are trying to understand how evaluations are developed and used within the organization. Finally, case studies provide appropriate recognition for those who were involved in the evaluation. They recognize the participants who achieved the results, as well as the managers who allowed the participants to be involved in the program. The case study format has become one of the most effective ways to learn about program evaluation. Exhibit 1.3 shows the ways in which case studies can be used.

Exhibit 1.3. Uses of Case Studies

Internal Uses of Case Studies	External Publication of Case Studies
Communicate results	Provide recognition to participants
Teach others	Improve image of functional unit
Build a history	Enhance brand of department
Serve as a template	Enhance image of organization
Make an impression	

A Case Example

Methods for communicating program results can be creatively combined to fit any situation. Here is an example that uses three approaches: case study, management meeting, and brochure.

The production unit of a major manufacturing company had achieved outstanding results through the efforts of a team of two supervisors. The results consisted of improvements in key measures such as absenteeism, turnover, lost-time accidents, grievances, scrap rate, and unit hour. The unit hour was a basic measure of individual productivity.

These results had been achieved through the efforts of the supervisors in applying the basic skills that they had been taught in a supervisor program—a fact that was mentioned at the beginning of a presentation made by the supervisors at a monthly meeting for all supervisors. In a panel discussion format with a moderator, the two supervisors outlined how they had achieved their results and answered questions. The comments were published in a brochure and distributed to all supervisors through their department managers. The title of the publication was "Getting Results: A Success Story." On the inside cover, specific results were detailed, along with additional information on the supervisors. A close-up photograph of each supervisor, taken during the panel discussion, was included on this page. The next two pages presented a summary of the techniques used to secure the results. The brochure was used in staff meetings as a discussion guide in order to cover the points from the panel discussion. Top executives were also sent copies of the brochure. In addition, the discussion was videotaped and used in subsequent programs as a model of how to apply skills. The brochure was used as a handout in those sessions.

The communication effort was a success. Favorable responses were received from all levels of management. Top executives asked the human resources development department to prepare and conduct similar meetings. Other supervisors began to use more of the skills and techniques presented by the two supervisors.

Process of Communication

Perhaps the greatest challenge of communication is the actual delivery of the message. Information can be communicated in a variety of ways and in many settings, depending on the target audience and the media selected for the message. Three practices deserve additional coverage. The first is relaying feedback data throughout a program so that necessary changes can be made. The second is presenting an impact study to a senior management team, which is one of the most challenging tasks for evaluators. The third is communicating regularly with the executive management group.

Providing Continual Feedback

One of the most important reasons for collecting reaction and learning data is to provide feedback so that adjustments or changes can be made throughout a program. In most programs, data are routinely collected and quickly communicated to the groups who need to know. Table 1.3 shows a feedback action plan designed to provide information to several feedback audiences, using a variety of media.

As the plan shows, data are collected during the program at four specific time intervals and communicated to at least four audiences: participants, team leaders, program team members, and the program sponsor. Some of these feedback sessions result in identification of specific actions that need to be taken. This process becomes wide-ranging and needs to be managed in a proactive way. We recommend the following guidelines for providing feedback and managing the feedback process (Block, 2000).

- *Communicate quickly.* Whether the news is good or bad, letting individuals involved in the program have the

Table 1.3. Feedback Action Plan

Data Collection Item	Timing	Feedback Audience	Media	Timing of Feedback	Action Required
1. Pre-program survey • Climate, environment • Issue identification	Beginning of the program	Participants Team leaders Program team Sponsor	Meeting Survey summary Survey summary Meeting	1 week 2 weeks 2 weeks 1 week	None None Communicate feedback Adjust approach
2. Implementation survey • Reaction to plans • Issue identification	Beginning of implementation	Participants Team leaders Program team Sponsor	Meeting Study summary Study summary Meeting	1 week 2 weeks 2 weeks 1 week	None None Communicate feedback Adjust approach
3. Implementation reaction survey or interviews • Reaction to solution • Suggested changes	1 month into implementation	Participants Support staff Team leaders Immediate managers Program team Sponsor	Meeting Survey summary Survey summary Study summary Study summary Meeting	1 week 2 weeks 2 weeks 2 weeks 3 weeks 3 days	Comments None None Support changes Support changes Adjust approach
4. Implementation feedback questionnaire • Reaction (planned action) • Barriers • Projected success	End of implementation	Participants Support staff Team leaders Immediate managers Program team Sponsor	Meeting Study summary Study summary Study summary Study summary Meeting	1 week 2 weeks 2 weeks 2 weeks 3 weeks 3 days	Comments None None Support changes Support changes Adjust approach

information as soon as possible is important. The recommended time for providing feedback is usually a matter of days, certainly no longer than a week or two after the results are known.

- *Simplify the data.* Condense the data into a concise, understandable presentation. This is not the time for detailed explanations and analysis.

- *Examine the role of the program team and the sponsor in the feedback situation.* On the one hand, sometimes the program team is the judge, jury, prosecutor, defendant, or witness. On the other hand, sometimes the sponsor is the judge, jury, prosecutor, defendant, or witness. The respective roles of the team and sponsor, in terms of their likely reactions to the data and the actions that need to be taken, should be examined.

- *Use negative data in a constructive way.* Some of the data will show that things are not going well, and the fault may rest with the program team or the sponsor. In either case, the story basically changes from "Let's look at the success we've had" to "Now we know which areas to change."

- *Use positive data in a conservative way.* Positive data can be misleading, and if they are communicated too enthusiastically, they may create expectations beyond what may materialize later. Positive data should be presented conservatively—with constraints and qualifiers outlined in detail.

- *Choose the language of the communication carefully.* Use language that is descriptive, focused, specific, short, and simple. Avoid language that is too judgmental, general, stereotypical, lengthy, or complex.

- *Ask the sponsor for reactions to the data.* After all, the sponsor is the customer, and the sponsor's reaction is critical.

- *Ask the sponsor for recommendations.* The sponsor may have some good recommendations about what needs to be changed to keep a program on track or to get it back on track if it has derailed.

- *Use support and confrontation carefully.* These two elements are not mutually exclusive. At times, support and confrontation may be needed for the same group. The sponsor may be confronted about lack of improvement or lack of active sponsorship yet may need support on those issues. Similarly, the program team may be confronted about problem areas but may require support as well.

- *React and act on the data.* Different alternatives and possibilities should be considered in order to arrive at the adjustments and changes to be made.

- *Secure agreement from all key stakeholders.* It is essential to ensure that everyone is willing to make the adjustments and changes that seem necessary.

- *Keep the feedback process short.* Don't let it become bogged down in long, drawn-out meetings or lengthy documents. If this occurs, stakeholders will avoid the process instead of being willing to participate in the future.

Following these guidelines will help you move your program forward and provide important feedback, often ensuring that adjustments are supported and made.

Presenting Impact Study Data to Senior Management

Perhaps one of the most challenging and stressful types of communication is the presentation of an impact study to the senior management team, which often is the sponsor of a program. The challenge is convincing this highly skeptical and critical group that outstanding results have been achieved (assuming that they have). The presenter needs to address the salient points and make sure the managers understand the evaluation process. Figure 1.1 shows our approach to presenting an impact study.

Two issues in particular can create challenges. First, if the results are impressive, convincing the managers to believe the data may be difficult. At the other extreme, if the data are negative, ensuring

Figure 1.1. Presenting an Impact Study to Executive Sponsors

Purpose of the Meeting
- Create awareness and understanding of ROI.
- Build support for the ROI Methodology.
- Communicate results of the ROI study.
- Drive improvement from results.
- Cultivate effective use of the ROI Methodology.

Guidelines for Conducting the Meeting
- Do not distribute the impact study until the end of the meeting.
- Be precise and to the point.
- Avoid jargon and unfamiliar terms.
- Spend less time on the lower levels of evaluation data.
- Present the data with a strategy in mind.

Presentation Sequence
1. Describe the program and explain why it is being evaluated.
2. Present the methodology.
3. Present the input and indicators.
4. Present the reaction and learning data.
5. Present the application data.
6. List the barriers to and enablers of success.
7. Present the business impact.
8. Show the monetary value of benefits.
9. Show the costs.
10. Present the ROI.
11. Show the intangibles.
12. Review the credibility of the data.
13. Summarize the conclusions.
14. Present the recommendations.

Figure 1.2. Streamlining Communication with Executives

First 2 ROI Studies	Detailed Study	Meeting
3–5 ROI Studies	Executive Summary	No Meeting
6 ROI Studies or More	One-Page Summary	No Meeting

that the managers don't overreact to the negative results and look for someone to blame can be a challenge.

The following guidelines can help you ensure that your presentation is planned and executed properly.

- Plan a face-to-face meeting with senior team members for the first one or two major impact studies, as shown in Figure 1.2. If the audience is unfamiliar with the ROI Methodology, a face-to-face meeting is necessary to make sure that they understand the process. The good news is that they will probably attend the meeting because they have not seen ROI data developed for programs or projects before. The bad news is that it takes a lot of time, usually an hour, for this presentation.

- After a group has had a face-to-face meeting for a couple of presentations, an executive summary may be all that is necessary for the next three to five studies. At this point, they understand the process, so a shortened version may be appropriate.

- After the target audience is familiar with the process, an even briefer version may be all that is needed; perhaps you can use a one- to two-page summary with charts or graphs showing all six types of measures. Exhibit 1.4 shows a one-page summary.

- During the initial face-to-face presentation, the results of the evaluation should not be distributed until the end of the session. This will allow the presenter to explain the evaluation process and obtain reactions to it before the target audience sees the actual ROI number.

- Present the process step by step, showing how the data were collected, when they were collected, who provided the data, how the data were isolated from other influences, and how they were converted to monetary values. Any assumptions, adjustments, and conservative approaches should be presented. Fully loaded costs should be presented so that the target audience will begin to buy into the process of developing the ROI.

- When the data are presented, the results should be presented step by step, beginning with Level 1, moving through Level 5, and ending with the intangibles. This sequence allows the audience to see the chain of impact from reaction and planned action to learning and confidence, application and implementation, business impact, and ROI. After some discussion of the meaning of the ROI, the intangible measures should be presented. Allocate time to each level as appropriate for the audience. This progression will help overcome potential negative reactions to a very positive or negative ROI.

- Show the consequences of additional accuracy, if it is an issue. The trade-off for more accuracy and validity is often more expense. Address this issue whenever necessary, agreeing to add more data if required.

Exhibit 1.4. Sample Streamlined Report

ROI Impact Study

Program Title: Preventing Sexual Harassment at Healthcare, Inc.

Target Audience: First- and second-level managers (655); secondary audience: all employees, through group meetings (6,844)

Duration: 1 day; 17 sessions

Techniques for Isolating the Effects of the Program: Trend line analysis; participant estimation

Techniques for Converting Data to Monetary Values: Historical costs; internal experts

Fully Loaded Program Costs: $277,987

Results

Level 1: Reaction	Level 2: Learning	Level 3: Application	Level 4: Impact	Level 5: ROI	Intangible Benefits
• 93% provided action items	• 65% increase in scores from pretest to posttest • Skill practice demonstration	• 96% conducted meetings and completed meeting record • 4.1 out of 5 overall average on behavior change survey • 68% report all action items complete • 92% report some action items complete	• Turnover reduction: $2,840,632 • Complaint reduction: $360,276 • Total improvement: $3,200,908	• 1,051%	• Job satisfaction • Reduced absenteeism • Stress reduction • Better recruiting

- Collect concerns, reactions, and issues with the process, and then make appropriate adjustments for the next presentation.

These steps will help you prepare and present your impact study, which is a critical step in the ROI Methodology.

Communicating with Executives and Sponsors

When you are communicating results, no group is more important than the top executives. In many situations, this group is also the sponsor. Improving communication with them requires developing an overall strategy, which may include some or all of the actions outlined in this section.

Strengthen the Relationship with Executives

An informal and productive relationship should be established between the manager responsible for the program evaluation and the top executive at the location where the program is being implemented. Each should feel comfortable with discussing needs and program results. One approach is to hold frequent informal meetings with the executive in order to review problems with current programs and discuss other performance problems or opportunities within the organization. Frank and open discussions may provide the executive with insight that is not available from any other source. Such discussions may also be very helpful to the program manager in determining the direction of the program.

Distribute Program Results

When a program has achieved significant results, inform the appropriate top executives by sending them a brief memo or summary outlining what the program was supposed to accomplish, when it was implemented, who was involved, and the results that were achieved. Use a for-your-information format that consists of facts rather than opinions. Keep it brief; a full report may be presented later. All significant communications on evaluation programs, plans, activities, and results should include the executive group. Frequent information on programs, as long as it is not boastful, can reinforce credibility and highlight accomplishments.

Ask Executives to Participate in Program Review

An effective way to increase commitment from top executives is to ask one or more of them to serve on a program review committee. A review committee provides input and advice to the program staff on a variety of issues, including needs, problems with current programs, and program evaluation issues. A program committee can be helpful in letting executives know about what programs are achieving.

Analysis of Reactions to Communication

The best indicator of how effectively the results of a program have been communicated is the level of commitment and support from the management group. Allocation of requested resources and strong commitment from top management are tangible evidence that management's perception of the results is positive. In addition to observing this macro-level reaction, the program team can use a few techniques to measure the effectiveness of its communication efforts.

Whenever results are communicated, the target audiences' reactions can be monitored. Their reactions may include nonverbal gestures, oral remarks, written comments, or indirect actions that reveal how the communication was received. Usually, when results are presented during a meeting, the presenter will have some indication of how the results were received by the group. The interest and attitudes of the audience can usually be quickly evaluated.

During the presentation, questions may be asked or, in some cases, the information may be challenged. A tabulation of these challenges and questions can be useful when the program team is evaluating the type of information to include in future communications. When positive comments about the results are made, formally or informally, they should also be noted and tabulated.

Staff meetings are an excellent arena for discussing the reaction to communications of results. Comments can come from many sources, depending on the target audience. Input from different members of the staff can be summarized to help judge the overall effectiveness of communications.

When major program results are communicated, a feedback questionnaire may be distributed to the audience or a sample of the audience. The purpose of this questionnaire is to determine the extent to which the audience understood or believed the information presented. Such a survey is practical only when the effectiveness of the communication will have a significant impact on future programs or actions.

Another approach is to survey the management group in order to determine its perceptions of the program results. Specific questions should be asked about the results. What does the management group know about the results? How believable are the results? What additional information is desired about the program? This type of survey can provide guidance for tailoring future communications.

The purpose of analyzing reactions is to make adjustments in the communication process—if adjustments are necessary. Although analyzing the reactions may involve intuitive assessments, a more sophisticated analysis will provide more accurate information, so that better adjustments can be made. The net result should be a more effective communication process.

Creating a Macro-Level Scorecard

In the last decade, organizations have shown growing interest in building a scorecard of the contributions of all programs within a function or organization. Sometimes, this is referred to as the *balanced scorecard* (Kaplan and Norton, 1996). A balanced scorecard includes data that represent a macro view and are balanced between qualitative and quantitative, customer and noncustomer, and financial and nonfinancial. Essentially, a scorecard is a group of measures that are important to the management team, and the management team takes action when the measures indicate a problem. Scorecards are a way to report the overall results of all programs within a function or all programs directed at a particular audience of executives and senior management.

Using the ROI Methodology, evaluations can be taken all the way to Level 5 (ROI), generating a scorecard of performance with seven types of data (including intangibles) for a program or project. A program scorecard is a micro-level scorecard (see Figure 1.3). To create a macro-level scorecard, micro-level scorecards are developed for all programs within a function or organization; every program usually has Level 0 (Inputs and Indicators) data and Level 1 (Reaction and Planned Action) data. Then, the micro-level evaluation data that were collected for each program are integrated into a macro-level scorecard, as illustrated in Figure 1.3. However, to keep the process effective and meaningful, only a few measures collected at Levels 0, 1, and 2 and data important to the management

Figure 1.3. Creating a Macro-Level Scorecard

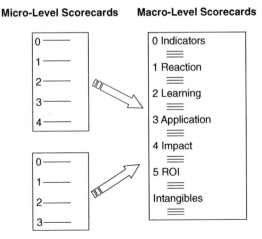

team are used at the macro level. For example, if a typical reaction questionnaire contains fifteen or twenty items, only four or five critical measures that are meaningful to the management group are chosen for each program. These critical measures are integrated into the macro-level scorecard. As each program is evaluated, measures are added to the overall scorecard.

Advantages of a Macro-Level Scorecard

A macro-level scorecard has several advantages. First, it provides a high-level view of a process or organizational function. For example, a macro-level scorecard for learning and development offers an overview of the activities, results, and contributions of the whole functional unit. Second, a macro-level scorecard provides a brief report on how the department is performing without the audience having to review detailed studies. Most executives prefer this type of report so they can have a bird's-eye view of how things are going overall. It is important to remember, however, that reviews of impact studies—or summaries of impact studies—of major programs and projects are also important. A simple scorecard won't do the trick in those cases.

Because some of the macro-level measures are linked to the business, a macro-level scorecard shows how programs connect to business objectives. A macro-level scorecard also provides a balanced perspective, offering activity, perception, qualitative, quantitative, application, and financial contribution measures. When used properly, this type of scorecard can indicate the alignment between an organization and a function. Thus, the macro-level scorecard can be an important tool for reporting results.

Example

Exhibit 1.5 shows a macro-level scorecard for a corporate university. In this example, thirty measures were collected, reflecting seven

Exhibit 1.5. An Example of a Corporate University Scorecard

First University

0. Indicators

    1. Number of Employees Involved

    2. Total Hours of Involvement

    3. Hours per Employee

    4. Training Investment as a Percentage of Payroll

    5. Cost per Participant

I. Reaction and Planned Action

    1. Percentage of Programs Evaluated at This Level

    2. Ratings on Seven Items Versus Targets

    3. Percentage with Action Plans

    4. Percentage with ROI Forecast

II. Learning

    1. Percentage of Programs Evaluated at This Level

    2. Types of Measurements

    3. Self-Assessment Ratings on Three Items Versus Targets

    4. Average Differences Between Pretest and Posttest Scores

III. Application

    1. Percentage of Programs Evaluated at This Level

    2. Ratings on Three Items Versus Targets

    3. Percentage of Action Plans Completed

    4. Barriers (List of Top Ten)

    5. Enablers (List of Top Ten)

    6. Management Support Profile

IV. Business Impact

    1. Percentage of Programs Evaluated at This Level

    2. Linkage with Measures (List of Top Ten)

    3. Types of Measurement Techniques

    4. Types of Methods to Isolate the Effects of Programs

    5. Investment Perception

V. ROI

    1. Percentage of Programs Evaluated at This Level

    2. ROI Summary for Each Study

    3. Methods of Converting Data to Monetary Values

    4. Fully Loaded Cost per Participant

    Intangibles

    1. List of Intangibles (Top Ten)

    2. How Intangibles Were Captured

levels of data: the six levels described in this series of books plus intangibles. Some of these measures need additional explanation. For example, at Level 1 (Reaction and Planned Action), for item 2, Ratings on Seven Items Versus Targets, seven specific measures were collected in every program. In practice, this firm used several Level 1 instruments (consisting of seven to twenty-one items). However, the seven measures on the macro scorecard were collected for every program. The seven measures included items such as relevance, importance, usefulness, and the amount of new material.

At Level 2 (Learning), self-assessments were administered to determine the participants' assessment of the learning that had taken place. The three metrics in item 3, Self-Assessment Ratings, involved the following items: "the extent to which I have learned the objectives of the program," "the extent to which I have learned all the materials presented during the program," and "the extent to which I have learned the skills and knowledge taught in the program." These measures can be taken for each program and integrated into the macro-level scorecard. When these data were collected each time, Level 2 measures were captured 100 percent of the time (item 1). In practice, some Level 2 measurements were much more detailed. There were objective tests, simulations, skill practices, and a variety of other measurement processes. The data from these detailed measurements were used to make adjustments in each program's design, development, and delivery; however, it would be difficult to integrate such detailed data into a macro-level scorecard. Therefore, some measurements were taken only for use in making adjustments in the program at the micro level, while other measurements were integrated into the macro-level scorecard.

Level 3 (Application) represents a rich source of data. Item 2, Ratings on Three Items Versus Targets, reflects the extent to which participants used the material, their success in the use of the material, and the frequency of use of the material. These three items can be collected in any type of program and therefore were collected as part of the follow-up process for all programs at this corporate university, then integrated into the macro-level score-card. The top ten barriers and the top ten enablers were taken directly from participants' forced-choice responses, providing evaluators with important information about which overall factors are helping and which are inhibiting success.

At Level 4 (Business Impact), item 2 requires explanation. As part of the follow-up evaluation for each program, the measures that matter to the organization were listed, and participants were given an opportunity to indicate the extent to which the program influenced each measure. Some integration rules were used on the data in order to determine the top ten measures that were influenced by the programs during a particular time frame. When these data were compared with the management team's priorities for the measures, the relationship between the programs and the overall business objectives was revealed.

At Level 5 (ROI) the data integration into the scorecard is relatively straightforward. ROIs on those programs evaluated to this level are reported. Methods for data conversion are listed and the fully loaded costs per participant. To complete the scorecard, intangible benefits are also listed. Additional information on developing a macro-level scorecard can be found at www.roiinstitute.net.

Final Thoughts

This chapter presents the final step in the ROI Methodology: communicating program results. Communicating results is a crucial step in the evaluation process. If this step is not taken seriously, the full impact of the results will not be realized.

This chapter covers some general principles for communicating program results and provides a framework of seven issues that should be addressed in any significant communication effort. Target audiences are discussed; the executive group is emphasized because it is the most important audience. A recommended format for a detailed evaluation report is provided. The chapter also presents details on the most commonly used media for communicating program results, including meetings, publications, electronic media, and macro-level scorecards.

References

Block, P. *Flawless Consulting.* (2nd ed.) San Francisco: Pfeiffer, 2000.

Kaplan, R., and Norton, D. *The Balanced Scorecard: Translating Strategy into Action.* Boston: Harvard Business School Press, 1996.

Making the Transition to the ROI Methodology

The best-designed methodology is still worthless if it is not integrated efficiently and effectively within an organization for which it was intended. Although the ROI Methodology presented in this series of books is a step-by-step, methodical, and simple procedure, in order for it to be applied successfully, it must be broadly incorporated and fully accepted and supported by those who must make it work. This chapter focuses on the critical issues involved in making the transition from an activity-based approach to a results-based approach through a comprehensive measurement and evaluation process.

Overcoming Resistance to the ROI Methodology

Any new process or change engenders resistance. Resistance appears in many ways: negative comments, inappropriate actions, or dysfunctional behaviors. Exhibit 2.1 lists some comments that might reflect open resistance to the ROI Methodology among staff members. Each comment represents an issue that must be resolved or addressed. A few of the comments are based on real barriers, while others are based on myths that must be dispelled. Sometimes, resistance to ROI reflects underlying concerns. The individuals involved may fear losing control. Others may feel that they could be vulnerable to actions that might be taken in response to unsuccessful

Exhibit 2.1. Typical Objections to the ROI Methodology

- This costs too much.

- This takes too much time.

- Who is asking for this?

- This is not listed in my job duties.

- I did not have input on this.

- I do not understand this.

- Is this a credible process?

- What happens when the results are negative?

- How will the data be used?

- How can we be consistent with this?

- The ROI process seems too subjective.

- Our managers will not support this.

- ROI is too narrowly focused.

- This is not practical.

- Who is responsible for this?

programs. Still others may be concerned about any process that requires additional learning and actions.

Members of all the major target audiences addressed in this book may resist the use of the ROI Methodology. Resistance may appear among the program staff, and they may make comments similar to those listed in Exhibit 2.1. Heavy persuasion and evidence of tangible benefits may be needed to convince individuals that the ROI Methodology should be implemented because it is in their best interest.

Another key player, the sponsor, may also resist. Although most sponsors want to see the results of an ROI evaluation, they may have concerns about the quality or accuracy of data. In addition, they may be concerned about the time commitments and the costs involved in conducting an ROI study.

The managers of participants in programs make up another group that may develop resistance. Managers may have concerns about the information they will be asked to provide and about how their performance will be judged along with that of the participants. They may express some of the fears listed in Exhibit 2.1.

The challenge is implementing the ROI Methodology methodically and consistently so that it becomes a routine and standard process that is built into the programs of an organization. Implementation of the ROI Methodology needs to include a detailed plan for overcoming the resistance to the process, for several reasons.

Resistance Is Always Present

There is always resistance to change. Sometimes there are good reasons for resistance, but often it exists for the wrong reasons. The important point is to sort out both types of resistance. When legitimate barriers are the basis for resistance, try to minimize them or remove them altogether.

Implementation Is Key

In any process, effective implementation is the key to its success. Implementation is successful when the new technique or tool is integrated into the routine framework of the function or organization. Without effective implementation, even the best process will fail. A process that is never removed from the shelf will never be understood, supported, or improved. A comprehensive implementation process with clear steps for overcoming resistance must be developed.

Consistency Is Necessary

As the ROI Methodology is implemented, consistency from one program evaluation to another is a critical consideration. With consistency come accuracy and reliability. The only way to ensure consistency is to follow clearly defined processes and procedures each time an ROI evaluation is conducted. Proper implementation will ensure that consistency occurs. Consistency can melt resistance.

Efficiency Is Always an Issue

Cost control and efficiency will always be an issue in any major undertaking, and using the ROI Methodology is no exception. The implementation process must ensure that tasks are completed efficiently as well as effectively, so that the costs associated with the process are kept to a minimum, time is used appropriately, and the process remains affordable.

The implementation process that is necessary to overcome resistance covers many areas. Figure 2.1 shows the actions outlined in this book that are the building blocks in overcoming resistance. They are all necessary, and together they form the base or framework for dispelling myths and removing or minimizing barriers. The remainder of this chapter presents specific strategies and techniques for performing each of the actions identified in Figure 2.1.

Transition Issues

After a decision has been made to introduce the ROI Methodology, it is important to review the resource issues that may arise from the changes and consider how to address them. Individuals frequently have different views on whether a change is needed, what drives it, and how much impact it will have. No one in an organization will support a results-based change effort without some understanding of

Figure 2.1. A Transition Plan: Building Blocks for Overcoming Resistance

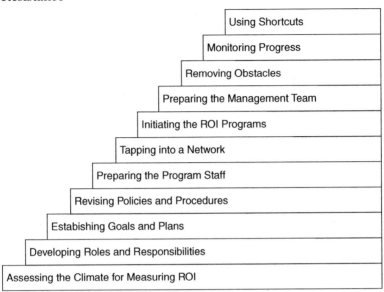

why the change is needed and what benefits it may produce. Implementing the ROI Methodology requires significant commitment, knowledge, and support across *all* organizational levels. Unless the purposes and desired outcomes are clear, it is unrealistic to expect others to invest time and effort in the process.

Recognizing long-term implementation of the ROI Methodology as a change effort is critical to addressing the transition challenges. Most executives, managers, or employees think of major organizational change in terms of reengineering, restructuring, or culture change. For the purposes of this book, change is the fundamental shift from an old state (activity-based measurement and evaluation) to another, transformed state (results-based measurement and evaluation). This shift will encompass reengineering the function or organization; restructuring policy, procedures, and practices; and influencing organizational culture in regard to the value of the organizational function and the role that executives,

Figure 2.2. Steps in Planning a Transition

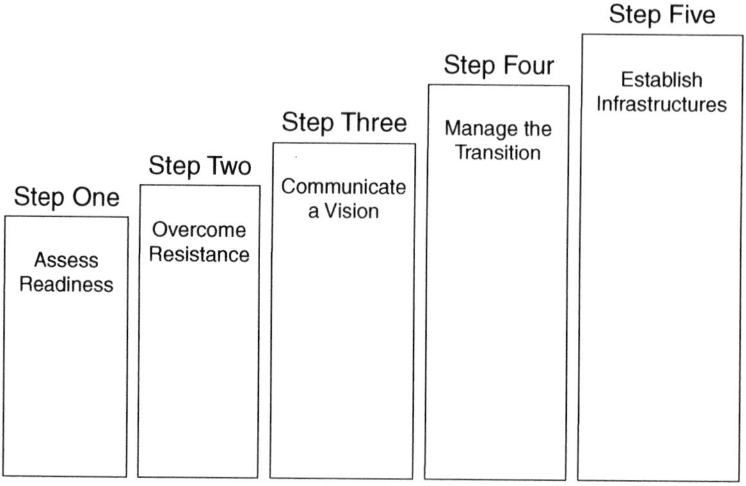

managers, and employees play in achieving performance results. Most change efforts involve more than one type of change. Given that context and scope, moving from an old to a new state is likely to be more successful when incremental transition-planning steps are applied.

Transition-Planning Steps

Proven steps in transition planning are illustrated in Figure 2.2. Each step comprises specific activities that reveal potential barriers to ROI readiness and help the organization identify areas of strength and opportunity in the implementation process.

Step 1: Assess Readiness

By some estimates, 70 to 75 percent of major organizational change efforts fail. Imagine the wasted time, money, and human effort that are represented by that dismal figure. If implementing organizational change is truly that difficult, then it is clear that planning, resource, and management needs have to be addressed from the very beginning. Time must be spent up front to assess the kinds of planning, resource, and management activities needed to support

ROI implementation efforts. Proper planning on the front end will save time and other resources on the back end.

Prior to undertaking a time-consuming, labor-intensive ROI evaluation, it would be prudent to assess perceptions and mindsets about evaluation within your organization, along with its readiness for the robust ROI Methodology. Completing the readiness assessment, "Is Your Organization a Candidate for Implementation of the ROI Methodology?" from *ROI Fundamentals*, book one in this series, will help you determine how best to focus organizational readiness activities. This assessment, along with the scale for determining if your organization is ready for the ROI Methodology, is shown in Exhibit 2.2.

Before implementation, the response to each of the fifteen statements in the assessment should be examined or reexamined in light of its potential effect on the effort to implement results-based measurement. For example, strong agreement with item 11 indicates an immediate need or opportunity to position implementation of the ROI Methodology as a compelling part of organizational strategy and then define the readiness conditions required to support it.

Using the responses from the readiness assessment, identify and prioritize key focus areas for readiness activities. In particular, consider the following:

- What programs, processes, or persons in your organization support the desired future state of measurement focus? (*Strengths*)

- Where are there gaps between where your organization is and where it should be with respect to results-based measurement? (*Weaknesses*)

- What processes or programs may have to be changed or reconfigured?

- To what extent do managers and program staff perceive current programs to be effective? (*Opportunities*)

Exhibit 2.2. Is Your Organization a Candidate for Implementation of the ROI Methodology?

Read each question and check the box that corresponds to the most appropriate level of agreement:

1 = Disagree; 5 = Agree

	DISAGREE 1	2	3	4	AGREE 5
1. My organization is considered a large organization with a variety of projects and programs.					
2. My function has a large budget that attracts the interest of senior management.					
3. My organization has a culture of measurement and is focused on establishing a variety of measures for all functions.					
4. My organization is undergoing significant change.					
5. There is pressure from senior management to measure the results of our programs.					
6. My function has a low investment in measurement and evaluation.					
7. My organization has experienced more than one program disaster in the past.					
8. My function has a new leader.					
9. My team would like to be the leader in evaluating programs and processes.					
10. The image of my function is less than satisfactory.					
11. My clients are demanding that programs and processes show bottom-line results.					

Exhibit 2.2. Is Your Organization a Candidate for Implementation of the ROI Methodology? (*Continued*)

12. My function competes with other functions in our organization for resources.					
13. Increased focus has been placed on linking programs and processes to the strategic direction of the organization.					
14. My function is a key player in change initiatives currently taking place in our organization.					
15. Our function's overall budget is growing, and we are required to prove the bottom-line value of our processes.					

Scoring
Add your score based on the level of agreement to each question. A score of "1" equals 1 point; a score of "5" equals 5 points.

If you scored:

15–30	Your organization is not yet a candidate for the ROI Methodology.
31–45	Your organization is not a strong candidate for the ROI Methodology. However, you should start pursuing some type of measurement process.
46–60	Your organization is a candidate for building skills to implement the ROI Methodology. At this point there is no real pressure to show ROI, which means that you have the perfect opportunity to put the ROI Methodology in place within your organization and perfect the process before it becomes a requirement.
61–75	Your organization should already be implementing a comprehensive measurement and evaluation process, including ROI calculations.

- What resource constraints may impede implementation? (*Threats*)

- What processes may have to be created from scratch?

- What particular areas need immediate support in order for implementation to proceed?

- What metrics, milestones, or status reports are needed to track and monitor progress on implementation?

Exhibit 2.3. SWOT Analysis of Organizational Readiness for Implementation of the ROI Methodology

Strengths	Weaknesses
✓	✓
✓	✓
✓	✓
✓	✓
Opportunities	**Threats**
✓	✓
✓	✓
✓	✓
✓	✓

Based on your review of the readiness assessment and deliberation on the preceding questions, complete a strengths, weaknesses, opportunities, and threats (SWOT) analysis of your organization's readiness for implementation of the ROI Methodology (see Exhibit 2.3).

When the SWOT analysis is completed, identify and prioritize key focus areas. Once this is complete, developing a readiness plan to address specific areas that will need attention or action during implementation should be much easier to do.

Step 2: Overcome Resistance

With any new process or change, resistance is typical, as we discussed earlier. The group that most often resists the ROI Methodology is the program staff, who are tasked with the design, development, delivery, and coordination of programs and with their evaluation. These individuals may perceive the implementation of ROI measurement as threatening or time-consuming or as an unwelcome intrusion on an already overloaded schedule of looming deadlines, multiple requests for service, and never-ending client demands. Many practitioners are also deterred from pursuing systematic evaluation efforts because of false assumptions about the cost and complexity of evaluating at the ROI level. Compounding these issues is the occasional misuse of measurement data as a corrective or fault-finding tool rather than a source of continuous improvement. Furthermore, environmental barriers are typically present in that most functions have not established the infrastructure and success criteria to support a results focus.

ROI Fundamentals, the first book in this series, discusses the many common myths, fears, and false assumptions about implementing the ROI Methodology. Some of the more prevalent myths, fears, and assumptions are listed in Table 2.1, along with approaches for eliminating resistance associated with these preconceived notions. Each approach for eliminating resistance is detailed in this book.

Exhibit 2.4 provides a checklist of common myths, fears, or false assumptions associated with implementing the ROI Methodology. Complete this exercise to determine how you can overcome resistance in your organization. First, identify the preconceived notions in your organization.

Step 3: Communicate a Vision

Organizational readiness can be enhanced by actively communicating the vision, mission, and desired outcomes of a results-focused evaluation and measurement strategy. The vision highlights the difference between the current reality of where the organization is with its measurement focus and where its leaders want it to be. Through communication forums or briefings with senior, mid-level, and line managers, the value of moving from an activity-based measurement focus to a results-based focus can be described and input can be gathered about how others view the change. These initial communications should be designed to help organizational leaders

Table 2.1. How to Overcome Myths, Fears, and False Assumptions About the ROI Methodology

Myth, Fear, or Assumption	Specific Approaches
1. Measurement and evaluation are too expensive.	• A comprehensive measurement and evaluation system can typically be implemented for less than 5 percent of a function unit's budget. • Benchmark with other organizations to determine a reasonable range for evaluation costs. For most programs, it is sufficient to collect learning and application data, so the cost of a detailed impact study is infrequent.
2. Evaluation takes too much time.	Take advantage of these proven shortcuts and cost-saving approaches: • Use automated techniques and templates. • Build evaluation into the performance improvement process. • Develop criteria for selecting program measurement levels. • Plan for evaluation early in the process. • Share the responsibilities for evaluation. • Require participants to conduct major steps. • Use shortcut methods for major steps. • Use estimates in the data collection and analysis. • Develop internal capability in the ROI Methodology. • Streamline the reporting process. • Use Web-based technology.

Table 2.1. How to Overcome Myths, Fears, and False
Assumptions About the ROI Methodology (*Continued*)

Myth, Fear, or Assumption	Specific Approaches
3. If senior management does not require additional measurement, there is no need to pursue it.	• Leaders are demanding more and more accountability. • A unit that produces no evidence of results becomes an easy target for staff reductions. • When senior leaders suddenly ask for results, they expect a quick response. • Having results available and not needing them is better than needing results and not having them. • Developing ROI information is one of the best ways to garner the respect of senior management and show the business value of a function.
4. Measurement and evaluation is a passing fad.	• Increased accountability and measurement are among the most critical issues today. • Although the status of ROI practice among professionals is mixed, there is a persistent trend toward showing the bottom-line value of program investments.
5. Evaluation generates only one or two types of data.	• The ROI Methodology can generate up to seven different types of qualitative and quantitative data, including intangible benefits.
6. Evaluation cannot be easily replicated.	• Follow the Twelve Guiding Principles and adopt operating standards in order to ensure consistency in using the ROI Methodology.

(*Continued*)

Table 2.1. How to Overcome Myths, Fears, and False
Assumptions About the ROI Methodology (*Continued*)

Myth, Fear, or Assumption	Specific Approaches
7. Evaluation is too subjective.	• The use of estimates is extremely reliable when sound operating standards are followed. • Accounting, engineering, and technology fields routinely use estimates.
8. Impact evaluation is not possible for programs involving soft skills; it is only possible for programs involving technical and hard skills.	• Hundreds of case studies document successful application of the ROI Methodology to soft-skill programs. • Link needs, objectives, and impact measures to identify performance improvement at Levels 3, 4, and 5.
9. Evaluation is more appropriate for certain types of organizations.	• The ROI Methodology has been successfully used by organizations of multiple sizes in diverse fields around the globe. • Impact measures that can be used to measure program success exist in any organizational setting.
10. Isolating the effects of a program is not always possible.	• Several methods for isolating the effects of a program are available; the challenge lies in selecting the appropriate method for a given situation. • Ignoring the isolation issue decreases the credibility of the function and makes linking the program to key business measures difficult.

Table 2.1. How to Overcome Myths, Fears, and False Assumptions About the ROI Methodology (Continued)

Myth, Fear, or Assumption	Specific Approaches
11. Because program staff have no control over participants after they complete a program, evaluating on-the-job improvement is not appropriate.	• Although the program staff may not have direct control over what happens to participants in the workplace, they do have influence on the process of transferring skills that participants will use in the workplace. • Objectives must be developed that focus on application of learning and expected outcomes. • Partnerships between key managers and program staff help ensure that learning transfer takes place.
12. A participant is rarely responsible for the failure of a program.	• Participants need to be held accountable for their own learning and are a credible source of information about the consequences of learning. • Programs need to be positioned with results-based expectations for participants. • Participants have the ultimate responsibility for learning and applying new skills and knowledge and for identifying enablers and barriers to their success in doing so.
13. Evaluation is the evaluator's responsibility.	Evaluation must be a shared responsibility: • Managers and performers provide input on performance and skill deficits. • Program team members design, develop, and deliver the program.

(Continued)

Table 2.1. How to Overcome Myths, Fears, and False Assumptions About the ROI Methodology (*Continued*)

Myth, Fear, or Assumption	Specific Approaches
	• Managers and stakeholders review and approve the evaluation plan. • Participants and key stakeholders provide data about success after the program.
14. Successful evaluation implementation requires a degree in statistics or evaluation.	• An effective, credible evaluation process can be implemented by means of a simple step-by-step process and without a complicated set of formulas. • Many evaluation studies do not require the use of statistics. • Statistical software packages can be purchased as a resource for evaluation staff, or statistical expertise can be hired for specific ROI impact studies.
15. Negative data are always bad news.	• Communicate a vision of the ROI Methodology as a continual learning tool that will help assess program priorities and areas of impact. • Develop staff capability in the ROI Methodology and share ownership of evaluation results.

understand the following points:

- Why the paradigm shift to a results-based measurement focus is needed

- What the desired outcomes are

- Who the targets for change are, and who is needed to make it work

Exhibit 2.4. Overcoming Resistance in the Form of Myths, Fears, and False Assumptions

A. For each item in the following list of common myths, fears, or false assumptions associated with implementing the ROI Methodology, check the box that reflects the mindset in your organization.		
Myth, Fear, or False Assumption	Yes	No
1. Measurement and evaluation are too expensive.	☐	☐
2. Evaluation takes too much time.	☐	☐
3. If senior management does not require additional measurement, there is no need to pursue it.	☐	☐
4. Measurement and evaluation is a passing fad.	☐	☐
5. Evaluation generates only one or two types of data.	☐	☐
6. Evaluation cannot be easily replicated.	☐	☐
7. Evaluation is too subjective.	☐	☐
8. Impact evaluation is not possible for programs involving soft skills; it is only possible for programs involving technical and hard skills.	☐	☐
9. Evaluation is more appropriate for certain types of organizations.	☐	☐
10. Isolating the effects of a program is not always possible.	☐	☐
11. Because program staff have no control over participants after they complete a program, evaluating the on-the-job improvement is not appropriate.	☐	☐

(Continued)

Exhibit 2.4. Overcoming Resistance in the Form of Myths, Fears, and False Assumptions (Continued)

12. A participant is rarely responsible for the failure of a program.	☐	☐
13. Evaluation is the evaluator's responsibility.	☐	☐
14. Successful evaluation implementation requires a degree in statistics or evaluation.	☐	☐
15. Negative data are always bad news.	☐	☐

B. Review the preceding list of objections associated with the ROI Methodology, and identify the three that *most* reflect your organization's current mindset about measurement and evaluation.

1. _____

2. _____

3. _____

C. Referring to the approaches listed in Table 2.1 for ideas, identify an action, strategy, or approach that you will use to counter each assumption listed in item B as your team completes an ROI impact study.

1. _____

2. _____

3. _____

D. Indicate the date by which you will complete each action listed in item C.

1. _____

2. _____

3. _____

E. Identify a person with whom you will share progress on each item.

1. _____

2. _____

3. _____

- When the impact will occur

- How a results-based function will align with the company's performance goals, vision, mission, and values

- How the organization, its internal processes, and its key people will be developed in order to manage the change effort

- Where the checkpoints will be and what process documents and project plans will detail the scope of the effort and its impact on the business

Communication should also include education about the components of a results-based measurement strategy, including the following:

- How evaluation data can be used to uncover barriers to successful application of skills or knowledge

- How the data can be used to manage and correct barriers

- The role of management in ensuring a program's success

- The role of top management in supporting data collection

- How a focus on results can save money and enhance business performance

The next chapter discusses management's role in implementing the ROI Methodology in more detail and provides additional tools for developing and strengthening partnerships with management groups. In communicating the vision for a results-based effort, however, it should be emphasized that results-based evaluation is not a quick fix and that successful implementation will require sustained support and participation across all organizational levels.

Communication with stakeholders typically acknowledges that implementation of a results-based evaluation framework is a gradual process.

Developing and maintaining a communication plan to promote awareness of and commitment to results-based evaluation is critical, not only for your current impact study but for future ROI efforts. Table 2.2 is an example of a communication plan. Exhibit 2.5 helps identify areas of strength and opportunities for improvement in existing communication work.

Step 4: Manage the Transition

As happens in many change efforts, people may underestimate the time, energy, and resources required to achieve evaluation goals. In fact, one of the most common errors made in any change effort is inaccurately defining the scope; typically, planners define the scope of the change effort too narrowly, overlooking the internal dynamics of day-to-day communications and working relationships. Imagine the losses of time and productivity that occur when those who must support and participate in a new evaluation strategy are unclear about their roles and the resources needed to support their roles. That's why defining roles and responsibilities is such an important part of transition planning and change management in the ROI Methodology. This essential step is discussed in more detail in Chapter Three.

Step 5: Establish Management Infrastructure to Support the Process

Systems, policies, and procedures ensure consistency in application of the ROI Methodology across an organization. They also keep the process focused, consistent, and credible by communicating how new approaches for measuring performance will be aligned with existing business processes and structures. Developing the proper infrastructure to support the ROI Methodology requires the following actions.

Table 2.2. Sample Communication Plan

Process: Results-Based Measurement and Evaluation							
Key Message	Stakeholder	Objective	Approach	Frequency	Responsibility	Delivery	Considerations
What is the primary message to be conveyed or issue to be addressed?	*Target audience*	*Info only, seeking support, requesting review, or action?*	*Web, newsletter, e-mail, face to face, hard copy, town hall, intranet, and so on*	*Timing or milestone date*	*Who will develop content?*	*Who will deliver the communication?*	*Potential obstacles, time availability, stakeholder concerns or issues with message*
Stage 1: Initial Rollout							
Value proposition of ROI and results-based measurement processes. Why, who, when, and how evaluation data will be used. Communicate best practices within the industry and the profession.	Senior leadership	Solicit support, resources for initial impact study.	Face-to-face PowerPoint presentation, including benchmarking data	One time, by [date]; ongoing, as needed	Process sponsor or program leader	Process sponsor or program leader	Why ROI? Why now? How to manage with limited resources? Should we do ROI for all programs? What will we do with the results? What about negative results? How can results of soft-skill programs be measured? How can we know whether it was the training that got the result?

(Continued)

Table 2.2. Sample Communication Plan (*Continued*)

Key Message	Stakeholder	Objective	Approach	Frequency	Responsibility	Delivery	Considerations
Emphasize focus on process, not a one-time-only initiative.	Senior leadership	Request technical review of revised policies and procedures as part of infrastructure needed to support results-based process.	Face-to-face PowerPoint presentation, including benchmarking data	One time, then ongoing as needed	Program leader	Process sponsor or program leader and initial evaluation team	Any conflict with existing critical business issues? Compatibility, synergies? Accountability measures.
Summary of current impact study. Show how ROI can be used to solve real business problems.	Senior leadership	Seek support for implementation plan. Generate accountability for mid-level managers', line supervisors', and employees' participation. Request documented support, with sign-off on data collection plan.	Face-to-face PowerPoint presentation, including benchmarking data; data collection plan	One time, then ongoing as needed	Process sponsor or program leader	Process sponsor or advisor	Amount of resources needed. Confidentiality of results. What will happen if results are negative or less than desirable?

Value proposition: how results-based measurement processes can solve real business problems.	Line supervisors	Seek support for implementation plan. Request line supervisors' involvement in task force. Request documented support, with sign-off on data collection plan.	Face-to-face PowerPoint presentation, including benchmarking data; data collection plan; transfer strategy matrix	One time, then ongoing as needed	Process sponsor or program leader	Process sponsor or advisor	Resource constraints? How will performance tracking be conducted? What impact will this have on performance management processes? What's in it for me? How will organizational or management barriers be addressed?
Value proposition: how results-based measurement processes can solve real business problems.	Employees, program participants	Seek support for implementation plan. Request documented support, with sign-off on data collection plan.	Face-to-face PowerPoint presentation, including benchmarking data; data collection plan; transfer strategy matrix	One time, then ongoing as needed	Process sponsor or program leader	Process sponsor or advisor	Resource constraints? How will performance tracking be conducted? What impact will this have on performance management processes? What's in it for me? How will organizational or management barriers be addressed?

(Continued)

Table 2.2. Sample Communication Plan (Continued)

Key Message	Stakeholder	Objective	Approach	Frequency	Responsibility	Delivery	Considerations
Stage 2: Evaluation Planning							
Explain business needs or gaps that are being addressed, in terms of current and desired performance levels. Discussion of performance measures available to track progress on objectives.	Line supervisors	Review extant baseline data; collect input for cause analysis, proposed performance improvement solution; establish evaluation targets with corresponding measures.	Face-to-face PowerPoint presentation, including benchmarking data; data collection plan; transfer strategy matrix	Weekly, as needed. Evaluation plan to be completed, with senior management input, by [date].	Evaluation lead, task force members, instructional design team rep, subject matter experts, participants	Evaluation lead, task force members, instructional design team rep, subject matter experts, participants	What about conflicting priorities? Moving targets?
Stage 3: Data Collection							
Solicit feedback about success on reaction, planned action, learning, performance, and impact objectives. Collect application and business measures of program impact.	Line supervisors	Request feedback during and after program implementation. Instruct participants on how to provide feedback. Gather input in order to convert data to monetary values and calculate ROI.		Per data collection plan, by [date]	Evaluation lead, task force members, instructional design team rep, subject matter experts, participants	Evaluation lead, task force members, instructional design team rep, subject matter experts, participants	What about extreme data? What about missing data? Standards for converting data and ensuring credibility? Confidentiality? Annualized data?

Solicit feedback about success on reaction, learning, action, performance, and impact objectives. Collect application and business measures of program impact.	Program participants	Request feedback during and after program implementation. Instruct participants on how to provide feedback. Gather input in order to convert data to monetary values and calculate ROI.	Level 1 feedback survey. Pre-program and post-program assessments. Action plan and impact survey sixty days after program.	Per data collection plan, by [date]	Evaluation lead, task force members, instructional design team rep, subject matter experts, participants	Evaluation lead, task force members, instructional design team rep, subject matter experts, participants	What about extreme data? What about missing data? Standards for converting data and ensuring credibility? Confidentiality? How can barriers in management support be reported? Annualized data?

Stage 4: Reporting Results

Report on degree of success in achieving program objectives. List enablers and barriers.	Senior and mid-level managers	Communicate results. Seek support for action planning, program revisions, or other improvements, as needed.	Town hall meetings. Impact study report. Lessons learned report.	Selected senior and mid-level management briefings. Two town hall forums by [date].	Sponsor, evaluation lead, task force members, subject matter experts, participants	Sponsor, evaluation lead, task force members, subject matter experts, participants	How will results be used for continuous improvement and action planning? How will issues of management support (or lack thereof) be addressed?

(Continued)

Table 2.2. Sample Communication Plan (*Continued*)

Key Message	Stakeholder	Objective	Approach	Frequency	Responsibility	Delivery	Considerations
Report on degree of success in achieving program objectives. List enablers and barriers.	Line supervisors	Communicate results. Seek support for future participation in impact studies and involvement in task force. Generate enthusiasm for process.	Briefings. Intranet communications. Poster boards. Lessons learned report.	Ongoing, as needed	Sponsor, evaluation lead, task force members, subject matter experts, participants	Sponsor, evaluation lead, task force members, subject matter experts, participants	How will results be used for continuous improvement and action planning? How will issues of management support (or lack thereof) be addressed?

Exhibit 2.5. Communication Planning

1. Using Table 2.2 as a guide, complete a communication plan for your current impact study. Next, use the checklist below to identify areas of strength and opportunities for improvement in your existing communication plan.		
Communication Planning Checklist	Yes	No
Have I checked with members of my target audience to assess communication needs, concerns, or questions?	☐	☐
Have I considered the organizational impact of a results-based focus?	☐	☐
Have I engaged the support of a credible sponsor at the senior leadership level?	☐	☐
Have I clarified the purpose of the results-based evaluation, what outcomes are desired, and what decisions will be made based on the results?	☐	☐
Have I used baseline data to support my case?	☐	☐
Have I positioned this effort as a compelling piece of company strategy?	☐	☐
Have I assessed external factors that may be out of the program staff's or individual client's control?	☐	☐
Have I developed an evaluation plan with program objectives at multiple levels?	☐	☐
Have I included communication about timelines and resource requirements?	☐	☐
Have I included communication about evaluation roles and responsibilities across all organization levels?	☐	☐
Have I included communication about how a results-based evaluation process will be integrated with existing policy and purpose statements?	☐	☐
Have I included a transition plan with realistic milestones?	☐	☐

(*Continued*)

Exhibit 2.5. Communication Planning (*Continued*)

Have I included communication about the data collection instruments to be used for measuring results in targeted areas?	☐	☐
Have I included clear communication about the resource requirements for stakeholders who participate in the evaluation process?	☐	☐
Have I included communication about accountability measures for stakeholders who commit to participation in the evaluation process?	☐	☐
Have I provided adequate communication about how participants will be trained to provide data?	☐	☐
Have I included communication about how results will be used for continuous improvement and action planning?	☐	☐

Areas of strength:

_____

_____

_____

Opportunities for improvement:

_____

_____

_____

2. Identify planned actions you will take to maintain and enhance communication efforts in the areas needing improvement.
Sustaining actions:

_____

_____

_____

Enhancing actions:

_____

_____

_____

Prepare Policy, Procedures, and Guidelines

As part of the integration process, operating policies, procedures, or standards concerning measurement and evaluation should be established or revised. For example, one organization used the following policy statement to frame the purpose of its results-based initiatives: "The purpose of workplace learning programs is to increase organizational, operational, and individual effectiveness. Programs will offer tangible and intangible returns to customers and will assist the company in addressing all factors influencing organizational, operational, and individual performance."

Policy statements should also address critical issues that will influence the effectiveness of the measurement and evaluation process. Policy statements are best developed with input from the program staff and key stakeholders or clients of programs and services. Typical topics include these:

- Adoption of an evaluation framework (such as the five-level model presented in this series)

- Requirements that some or all programs set performance or business impact objectives

- Definition of roles and responsibilities

Policy statements provide an excellent opportunity to communicate basic evaluation requirements, including accountability requirements for those responsible for carrying out the evaluation process. Exhibit 2.6 provides a list of topics to include when you are updating organizational policy statements to better reflect a results-based strategy.

Guidelines tend to be more technical and detailed than policy statements and are meant to show how aspects of a results-based policy are undertaken and put into practice. They often include specific forms, instruments, and tools that are necessary to facilitate the process.

Exhibit 2.6. Checklist of Topics for Policy Statements

Policy Statement	Yes	No
Purpose of results-based measurement and evaluation strategy stated?	☐	☐
Purpose aligned with compelling business strategy?	☐	☐
Evaluation framework stated?	☐	☐
Evaluation process clearly linked with the entire performance improvement cycle, beginning with needs analysis and ending with communicating results?	☐	☐
Evaluation targets stated (that is, percentage of programs to be evaluated at Level 3 and above)?	☐	☐
Evaluation responsibilities stated for participants, managers, program staff, and stakeholders?	☐	☐
Standards for developing, applying, and ensuring the credibility of data collection instruments addressed?	☐	☐
Required capabilities for internal and external measurement staff stated?	☐	☐
Administrative and database issues addressed?	☐	☐
Criteria for communicating evaluation results stated?	☐	☐
Process of reviewing evaluation data for purposes of continuous improvement explained?	☐	☐

Exhibit 2.7 shows how one learning and development department applied a corporate template for business process development to its efforts to standardize results-based processes as credible business practices throughout the organization. In this example, policy statements are referenced as supporting documentation.

Exhibit 2.7. Learning and Development Standardization Process

Contents

1.0 Process Overview

2.0 Procedures

3.0 Resources, Roles, and Responsibilities

4.0 Measurement and Verification

5.0 Continual Improvement

6.0 Document Control Information

7.0 Document List

1.0 Process Overview

1.1 Purpose and Objective

Develop, approve, and deploy standardized learning and development (L&D) processes that are capable of enhancing and improving operational performance.

1.2 Scope

These L&D standardization processes will establish specific, mandatory requirements related to learning throughout the organization and will also contain additional guidelines to help business units meet the intent of the L&D standardization expectations. The process includes

- Governance

- Process development

- Training for governance team members and key L&D process implementers

Exhibit 2.7. Learning and Development Standardization Process (*Continued*)

1.3 Link to Operational Goals

This process facilitates meeting operational goals of excellence throughout the organization.

1.4 Process Requirements

1. All L&D processes will be consistent with
   - The company's way
   - The company's mission, vision, and values

2. A development team will manage the creation of the initial set of L&D standardized processes.

3. L&D standardized processes will be developed using a team approach, with membership that includes subject matter experts and representatives from select business units.

4. L&D standardized processes will be benchmarked against recognized best practices and industry leaders in L&D to ensure that the company processes are capable of delivering the intended objectives.

5. L&D standardized processes will be reviewed and approved by critical stakeholders before finalization.

6. A review council will examine final L&D standardized processes for business alignment and fitness for purpose.

7. An approval board will ensure that L&D standardized processes align with the company's strategic plan and that significant implementation issues and business impact have been accounted for.

8. Each L&D standardized process will be deployed with an implementation plan that identifies and gives guidance on significant implementation issues, such as communication, resource planning, and alignment with operational excellence (OE) strategies.

Exhibit 2.7. Learning and Development Standardization Process (*Continued*)

---

9. An exception procedure will be available for use by business units and departments in cases in which they feel that they cannot comply with a specific L&D process requirement or that compliance would not make business sense.

1.5 Links to Other Operational Processes

L&D standardization supports all other appropriate business processes, such as annual business planning, performance appraisal cycles, and individual development planning processes.

2.0 Procedures

2.1 Overview

A governance model will be used to develop, review, and approve L&D processes. The governance model has four representative components, including the following:

- Process sponsor to provide executive leadership and allocate resources for process implementation.

- Process champion to provide L&D technical expertise, mentoring, and training for process development team members and organizational stakeholders.

- Process development team to revise, write, and implement L&D processes. This plan will identify significant implementation issues and give guidance on approaches and timing.

- Process review council to examine processes to ensure fitness for purpose and alignment with business plans and give final approval.

Exhibit 2.7. Learning and Development Standardization Process (*Continued*)

2.2 Details of Governance

2.2.1 Governance—Process Sponsor Charter

Description: This charter describes process sponsorship roles, responsibilities, and procedures used for scheduling, resourcing, and soliciting stakeholder engagement in L&D standardized process development.

2.2.2 Governance—Process Champion Charter

Description: This charter describes process champion roles, responsibilities, and procedures used for advising, resourcing, and training process development team members and organizational stakeholders.

2.2.3 Governance—Process Development Team Charter

Description: This charter describes team membership, roles, responsibilities, and procedures used for scheduling, resourcing, writing, and soliciting input and approval for L&D standardized processes.

2.2.4 Governance—Review Council Charter

Description: This charter describes team membership, roles, responsibilities, and procedures used for advising on overall priorities and reviewing and approving the L&D standardized processes.

2.3 Components of Process Development

2.3.1 L&D Processes—Terms and Definitions

2.3.2 Purpose and Scope Statements

Exhibit 2.7. Learning and Development Standardization Process (Continued)

2.3.3 Process Development Procedures

2.3.4 Process Development Flowchart

2.3.5 Process Approval Procedure

3.0 Resources, Roles, and Responsibilities

L&D standardization process sponsor:	Name(s), Title
L&D standardization process champion:	Name(s), Title
L&D standardization process development team:	Name(s), Title
L&D standardization process review council:	Name(s), Title

The following table outlines the roles and responsibilities associated with this process.

Role	Responsibilities	Competencies
L&D standardization process sponsor	• Provides executive leadership for the L&D standardization process integration • Ensures that this process is kept current • Allocates personnel, funding, and other resources to support process execution • Reviews standardization process documentation and records • Participates in an annual review of process effectiveness and efficiency	• Fluency in operational excellence • Comprehensive knowledge of all elements of a results-based L&D focus, including understanding of the five-level measurement and evaluation framework • Ability to provide vision and strategic direction

(Continued)

Exhibit 2.7. Learning and Development Standardization Process (Continued)

Role	Responsibilities	Competencies
L&D standardization process champion	• Provides subject matter expertise and technical assistance for process development and execution • Ensures that processes adhere to operating standards, policies, and guidelines • Conducts performance reporting and trend analysis company-wide • Facilitates organization-wide changes in L&D process methodology • Mentors, trains, and manages the internal L&D and/or ROI community of practice	• Extensive experience and comprehensive knowledge of best-practice L&D processes, including results-based learning and ROI process models • Facilitative skills • Ability to evaluate results against organizational goals • Data analysis/interpretation skills • Strong business acumen, including understanding of operational excellence (OE) components • Demonstrated performance-consulting skills • Influencing skills
L&D standardization process development team members	• Described in the development team charter	• Influencing skills • Technical subject matter expertise • Understanding of internal business unit networks

Exhibit 2.7. Learning and Development Standardization Process (*Continued*)

Role	Responsibilities	Competencies
		• Understanding of continual improvement • Understanding of OE components • Strong communication skills
Review council members	• Described in the review council charter	• Fluency in OE components • Ability to provide vision and strategic direction • Understanding of the L&D standardization process • Understanding of business impact of deploying L&D standardization processes

4.0 Measurement and Verification

4.1 Measurement of L&D Effectiveness

Phillips's five-level framework and ROI process model will be used to measure L&D effectiveness across multiple levels of results. The following metrics will be tracked to determine that the L&D standardization process is effective in meeting its stated purpose. Measures will include:

Exhibit 2.7. Learning and Development Standardization Process (*Continued*)

4.1.1 Leading Measures

4.1.2 Lagging Measures

4.2 Verification

The following steps will be conducted to measure and verify that L&D processes, services, and products operate within defined standards of performance.

4.2.1 Review of Process Effectiveness

The L&D standardization process sponsor and process champion will review and verify that all parts of the L&D process are effective in fulfilling the OE expectations and results-based process purpose. The review will be performed annually, at a minimum.

4.2.2 Audit of Performance

The L&D standardization process sponsor and process champion will verify adherence and identify non-conformance to the L&D processes as designed and documented. A documented audit of the processes will occur at least annually and will be based on the following:

- Documents and records

- Demonstrated competence across five levels of L&D performance measures

- Process leading and lagging metrics

- Benchmarking data, if applicable

Exhibit 2.7. Learning and Development Standardization Process (*Continued*)

4.2.3 Governance Body Reviews

Governance bodies will perform the following reviews:

- Under the direction and guidance of the L&D standardization process sponsor and the process champion, the review council will evaluate the performance of the process development team annually.

5.0 Continual Improvement

The following steps will be conducted to assess and improve process performance.

5.1 Review of Process Effectiveness

The L&D standardization process sponsor and process champion will review and verify that all parts of the L&D processes are effective in fulfilling the operational expectations and results-based process purpose. The review will be performed at least annually.

5.2 Audit of Performance

The L&D standardization process sponsor and process champion will verify adherence and identify non-conformance to L&D processes as designed and documented. A documented audit of these processes will occur at least annually and will be based on the following:

- Documents and records

- Adherence to documented operating standards, policies, and guidelines

Exhibit 2.7. Learning and Development Standardization Process (*Continued*)

- Demonstrated competence across five levels of L&D performance measures

- Process leading and lagging metrics

- Benchmarking data, if applicable

5.3 Governance Body Reviews

Governance bodies will perform the following reviews:

- The review council will perform annual reviews to ensure appropriate progress toward implementation of the L&D processes throughout the organization.

- The review council will evaluate the performance of the process development team annually.

- The process sponsor will evaluate the performance of the review council annually.

5.4 Gap Analysis

The L&D standardization process sponsor, process champion, and development team will prioritize performance gaps and non-conformities that are identified as part of the process improvement step. Considerations will include operational directives, deviations from standard operating procedures, risk issues, and resource enablers/barriers.

5.5 Continual Improvement Plans

Process gaps, non-conformance, and improvement opportunities identified from 5.4 will be summarized and used to assist in building continual improvement plans.

Exhibit 2.7. Learning and Development Standardization Process (*Continued*)

5.6 Link to Annual Business Plan

The L&D standardization process champion and development team will use the prioritized performance gaps and non-conformities to develop a continual improvement plan that is linked with annual business plans. In some circumstances, improvement activities may extend over several years.

5.7 Contents

The continual improvement plan for OE processes will identify the following:

- Improvement opportunities and gaps to be closed
- Resources required
- Responsible person(s)
- Timing and milestones for improvements

6.0 Document Control Information

Revision dates, frequency of revisions, and control numbers should be recorded to ensure that only the most recently updated documents are used.

Description	Policy and Procedure Statement
Revision Date	
Revision Frequency	Every 3 years
Control Number	

Exhibit 2.7. Learning and Development Standardization Process (*Continued*)

7.0 Document List

This is a complete list of the documents referenced in this process.

- Five-Level Framework for Measuring L&D Results

- ROI Process Model

    Selection matrix

    Sample data collection plan

    Sample ROI analysis plan

- Sample Client Engagement and Service Level Agreement

- L&D Policy, Procedures, and Guidelines, including Operating Standards for L&D Measurement and Evaluation

- L&D Standardization Process Sponsor Charter

- L&D Standardization Process Champion Charter

- L&D Standardization Process Development Team Charter

- L&D Standardization Process Review Council Charter

- Glossary of Terms and Definitions

Defining operating standards for the ROI Methodology that will stand up under scrutiny is important. Again, operating standards are needed to ensure that practice is consistent and conservative from one staff member to the next and from one evaluation to the next. When you are developing and communicating operating standards for the ROI Methodology, follow these guidelines:

- *Report the complete story.* ROI is a critical measure, but it is only one of many types of data generated by the ROI Methodology. When a program is implemented, evaluate participant reaction, the extent to which participants improved their knowledge, how well participants applied the skills, and the business impact. If measurements are not taken at all levels, concluding that the results are due to the program is difficult.

- *Enhance credibility*. Using the most credible source (often the participants) will enhance stakeholders' perception of the quality and accuracy of the data analysis and results.

- *Be conservative*. If multiple options are available, select the most conservative data. This choice lowers the ROI but builds credibility.

- *Account for other factors*. Because the ROI Methodology is implemented as a systems approach, you must account for other factors in the environment that may have helped or hindered the results. At least one method should be used to isolate a program's effects. These methods are detailed in *Isolation of Results*, book three of this series. Without some method of isolation, the evaluation results will be inaccurate and overstated. Isolation strategies include comparing a pilot group that participated in a program to a control group that did not participate in the program; forecasting results without the program and then comparing the forecast to post-program results; and using participants' estimates of the influence of a program on key measures.

- *Account for missing data*. Sometimes, program participants leave the organization or change job functions. If participants cannot provide post-program improvement data, assume that little or no improvement has occurred. Making assumptions about improvements without data to back them up damages the credibility of the evaluation.

- *Adjust estimates for error.* Using estimates in reporting financial and benefit-cost information is common. To enhance the credibility of estimated data, the estimates should be adjusted according to the level of confidence in the data.

- *Omit the extremes.* Extreme data items can skew results, so omit them.

- *Capture annual benefits.* Use only the first year of benefits of short-term programs. If benefits are not quickly realized, they are probably not worth the cost. Reserve multiple-year ROI analyses for more extensive programs.

- *Tabulate all program costs.* The ROI must include all costs associated with a program. Omitting or understating costs will destroy the credibility of ROI results.

Collectively, these guidelines will do much to overcome resistance and convince stakeholders that the ROI Methodology is credible and that it produces accurate values and consistent outcomes.

Structure ROI as a Learning Tool, Not a Performance Evaluation Tool

A common reason program staff may resist the ROI Methodology is that they fear evaluation results will be used to highlight personal or program failures. For this reason, policies and guidelines should be used as a framework in order to position the ROI Methodology as a continuous process improvement tool that can help assess whether programs are meeting their objectives and proving their worth.

Develop a Project Plan

An important part of transition planning is establishing a project plan, as shown in Exhibit 2.8. Having a project plan is helpful for tracking progress toward goals and for identifying specific

Exhibit 2.8. Project Plan

Program: _____

Description: _____

Duration: _____ No. Participants: _____ Begin Date: _____ End Date: _____

	J	F	M	A	M	J	J	A	S	O	N	D
Formation of Evaluation Team												
Team member 1												
Team member 2												
Evaluation Planning												
Develop data collection plan												
Develop data collection instruments												
Design												
Test												
Revise												
Data collection administration plan												
Data Collection												
Implement data collection plan												
Collect responses												
Distribute incentives (see data collection administration plan)												

(Continued)

Exhibit 2.8. Project Plan (*Continued*)

Program: _____

Description: _____

Duration: _____ No. Participants: _____ Begin Date: _____ End Date: _____

	J	F	M	A	M	J	J	A	S	O	N	D
Data Analysis												
Develop ROI analysis plan												
Develop cost profile												
Analyze data												
Communication of Results												
Develop communication report												
Report results to Stakeholder Group 1												
Report results to Stakeholder Group 2												
Report results to Stakeholder Group 3												
Evaluation Follow-Up												
Develop steps to be taken to improve program												
Respond to questions from stakeholders												

individuals, timetables, milestones, and deliverables required to initiate and implement the evaluation process. The project plan is a fluid document, yet it serves as the master plan for the completion of the action items necessary to implement the evaluation process. Exhibit 2.9 presents a results-based transition plan.

Integrate Cost-Saving Methods

Some of the more common organizational concerns about implementing the ROI Methodology focus on the costs, time, and human resources required for the process. A department with limited time and resources can use proven shortcut methods to economize on major steps in the evaluation process. This provides a practical way to make the transition to the ROI Methodology and addresses resistance that may arise because of concerns about resource requirements. Figure 2.3 shows how these cost-saving approaches can be used in implementation of the ROI Methodology.

Final Thoughts

Making the transition to the ROI Methodology typically includes these challenges:

- False assumptions, myths, or fears about the process

- Resistance to change

- Real or imagined resource constraints

- Limited infrastructure to support a results-based focus

Concerns about the cost, time, and resources required to show results certainly have merit. In business climates that increasingly demand more results from fewer resources, many leaders may have to leverage existing resources and compete for the additional resources needed to demonstrate a program's bottom-line value. Exhibit 2.10 provides a summary of some cost-saving approaches.

Exhibit 2.9. Results-Based Transition Plan

Key Tasks	Milestone	1st Quarter											
		Jan 9	Jan 16	Jan 23	Jan 30	Feb 6	Feb 13	Feb 20	Feb 27	Mar 6	Mar 13	Mar 20	Mar 27
Form measurement team													
Assess stakeholder engagement opportunities													
Recruit process sponsor													
Deliver internal awareness presentations													
Develop measurement policy, guidelines													
Define operating standards													
Conduct internal readiness assessment													
Set evaluation targets, with stakeholder input													
Define roles and responsibilities													

Identify business critical priorities and "quick wins" • Identify ROI Project 1 • Identify ROI Project 2									
Develop scorecard framework									
Develop communication plan									
Provide professional development training for internal staff									
Train supplier partners									
Revise RFP guidelines									
Provide management, executive briefings									
Acquire or develop support tools									
Develop sustaining mechanisms (that is, standardization processes)									
Present impact study results (internally and externally)									

Figure 2.3. Cost-Saving Approaches to Implementation of the ROI Methodology

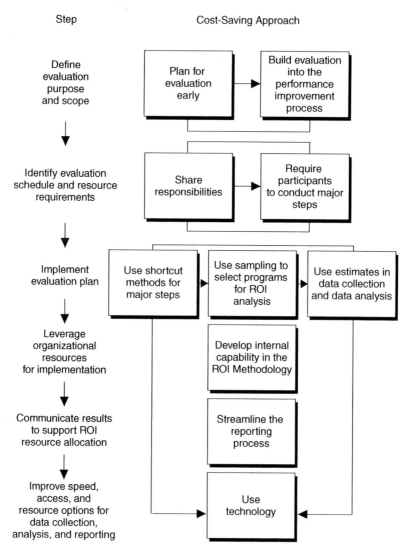

Exhibit 2.10. Cost-Saving Approaches to Implementation of the ROI Methodology

Approach 1: Plan for evaluation early in the process.

Guidelines: Define business needs, establish evaluation purposes, determine evaluation levels, develop project objectives, and determine evaluation timing.

Tools: Data collection plan, ROI analysis plan

Approach 2: Build evaluation into the process.

Guidelines: Link business needs, program objectives, and evaluation targets throughout the entire cycle of the needs assessment, instructional design, program delivery, and evaluation. Establish an infrastructure of evaluation policies, procedures, guidelines, and operating standards.

Tools: Linking needs to objectives and evaluation, policies, and procedures

Approach 3: Share responsibilities for evaluation.

Guidelines: Invite managers and employees to provide input on performance and skill deficits; ask stakeholders to review and approve evaluation plans; collect feedback data from participants and key stakeholders after the program.

Tools: Transfer approach matrix, management involvement checklist

Approach 4: Require participants to conduct major steps.

Guideline: Hold participants accountable for learning, applying new skills and knowledge, and identifying enablers and barriers to planned application of learning.

Tool: Action plan

Approach 5: Use shortcut methods for major steps.

Guidelines: Use just-in-time solutions for gap analysis, solution design, and data collection. Caution against an overreliance on shortcut methods and a quick-fix mentality.

Tool: Impact questionnaire

(Continued)

Exhibit 2.10. Cost-Saving Approaches to Implementation of the ROI Methodology (Continued)

Approach 6: Use sampling to select the most appropriate programs for ROI analysis.

Guidelines: Specific types of programs should be selected for a comprehensive, detailed analysis. Set targets for the number of programs to be evaluated at each level.

Tool: Matrix of selection criteria

Approach 7: Use estimates in data collection and data analysis.

Guidelines: Using estimates can save a great deal of time and money in the isolation and data conversion steps. Use the most credible and reliable sources for estimates, take a conservative approach, and develop a culture that accepts the estimation process.

Tools: Reaction and impact questionnaires, action plans

Approach 8: Develop internal capability in the ROI Methodology.

Guidelines: Communicate the purpose and scope of the ROI Methodology as a continuous improvement tool that will help assess program priorities and areas of impact. Develop staff capability and shared ownership through education and training and targeted development plans.

Tools: Management briefing outline, individual development plan

Approach 9: Streamline the reporting process.

Guideline: Once management is comfortable with ROI evaluations and a results-based measurement focus has been integrated into the organization, a streamlined approach to reporting results may be more appropriate and cost-effective.

Tool: Streamlined impact study template

Approach 10: Use technology.

Guidelines: Use suitable software packages to speed up various aspects of ROI analysis, design, evaluation, and reporting. Use technology to increase internal capability by offering online needs assessments, self-assessments, or evaluation templates for key stakeholders.

Tools: KnowledgeAdvisors' Metrics that Matter, Apian's SurveyPro, Gaelstorm's SenseiROI, iDNA's Audience Response System, Meeting Metrics Survey Tool, nTag Electronic Name Tags and Survey Tool, eePulse Assessment

Achieving a results-based evaluation strategy can be time-consuming and labor-intensive; in addition, it can be perceived as threatening. Yet with proper transitional planning and clearly defined, shared responsibilities, the ROI Methodology can be implemented in a proactive, systematic manner. Transition planning should allow for the fact that business alignment is still a new process for most managers and that the implementation of a results-based culture evolves over time. Assessing and creating individual and organizational readiness for implementation of the ROI Methodology is a vital step toward establishing business partnerships that will increase commitment to performance improvement programs going forward.

In this chapter, we see implementation of the ROI Methodology as an iterative change process and emphasize the importance of transition planning as a way of moving toward long-term integration of the process into the mainstream of the organization. Transition-planning steps, guidelines, and tools are provided in order to facilitate this effort.

The best-designed tools and techniques for implementation of the ROI Methodology are meaningless unless they are integrated into the fabric of an organization and accepted by those responsible for making it work. An evaluation champion and change agent is necessary for successful implementation. Organizational readiness and resistance to change should be routinely assessed. Objections should be addressed, responsibilities for results assigned, and a transition plan for measuring progress developed. The evaluation champion must commit to teaching others. The next chapter focuses on the role of the evaluation champion and on building capability and support for implementing the ROI Methodology.

3

Building Capability and Support

The preceding chapter discusses implementation of the ROI Methodology as a transitional change process and emphasizes the importance of addressing objections as part of effective transition planning. In this chapter we will focus on assigning responsibilities for results and on teaching others in order to build capability in the ROI Methodology. Implementing results-based evaluation strategies requires support from an infrastructure of diverse stakeholders whose complex interactions are structured by an array of reporting relationships. Because many individuals assume multiple or shifting roles in an evaluation effort, a major implementation challenge is identifying the right people, getting them involved, gaining their commitment, and keeping them well informed at all stages of the process.

Engaging the participation and commitment of different management groups is also a critical component of building internal capability and support for the ROI Methodology. Because managers must approve the time and resource allocations for all phases of implementation—including planning, data collection and analysis, and communication of results—addressing their unique needs and concerns poses special challenges.

Few initiatives are successful without the support and commitment of those involved in making them happen, and implementation of the ROI Methodology is no different. This chapter outlines approaches for creating shared ownership of implementation of the ROI Methodology for both the short term and the long term.

Fundamental Issues in Implementing the ROI Methodology

Educating stakeholders, managers, and responsible internal parties will provide them with a thorough understanding of evaluation using the ROI Methodology, promote consistency in its use, and ensure a common organizational language in regard to its application. Consistency is required, for with consistency come accuracy and credibility from one impact study to another and from one practitioner to the next. Staff members must be provided with consistent preparation for each step of the ROI Methodology.

Preparation of internal staff is a critical issue that must be addressed as part of implementation planning for the following reasons:

- Effective and consistent implementation requires capable and knowledgeable practitioners who can deliver on the promise of the ROI Methodology.

- Skill development in measurement and evaluation is not always a formal part of becoming a facilitator, instructional designer, performance improvement specialist, organizational effectiveness consultant, or manager.

- Effective development is key to increasing internal capability in the ROI Methodology.

Given the need to support implementation across all organizational levels, it may be helpful to identify key gaps as well as engagement opportunities as a first step toward developing internal capability in the ROI Methodology. This assessment of gaps and opportunities will help you pinpoint critical business partners with whom to apply the engagement and skill-building tactics described in this chapter. It can also help program teams identify where to leverage internal resources in order to

- Promote results-based measurement objectives

- Develop organizational understanding about the business value of a results-based process

- Create support for resource allocation

- Build organizational commitment to ensure implementation success

Identifying a Champion

Early in the implementation process, one or more individuals should be designated as the internal leader (or leaders) of the ROI Methodology implementation. As in most change efforts, someone must take the responsibility for ensuring that implementation is successful. This leader will champion the ROI Methodology; he or she should be the individual who understands the process best and has a vision of its potential contribution to the organization. More important, this leader should be willing to show and teach the methodology and its benefits to others.

Being the ROI leader is usually a full-time responsibility for a staff member in a large organization or a part-time one for someone in a small organization. The typical job title for a full-time ROI leader is manager of measurement and evaluation. Some organizations assign this responsibility to a team and empower this group to lead the implementation effort. In essence, team members are the champions for the ROI Methodology in their respective areas. For example, at Wachovia, one of the largest U.S. financial institutions, a task force of twenty-six professionals was selected, and each member became certified in the ROI Methodology and acted as a champion in his or her specific business unit. The vice president of assessment, measurement, and evaluation served as the chair of the team—the ROI leader.

Developing the ROI Leader

In preparation for the assignment of the ROI leader, an individual usually receives special training to build specific skills and knowledge in the ROI process. The role of the ROI leader is broad and fulfills a variety of specialized duties. The leader can take on many roles, as shown in Exhibit 3.1.

At times, the ROI leader serves as a technical expert, providing advice and making decisions about some of the issues involved in evaluation design, data analysis, and presentation. As an initiator, the leader identifies programs for ROI analysis and takes the lead in conducting the ROI studies. When needed, the leader is a cheer-leader, bringing attention to the ROI Methodology, encouraging others to become involved, and showing how the methodology can add value to the organization. Finally, the ROI leader is a commu-nicator, letting others know about the process and communicating results to a variety of target audiences. All the roles can come into play at one time or another as the leader implements the ROI Methodology within an organization.

The role of the ROI leader is a difficult and challenging one that will need special preparation and skill building. In the past,

Exhibit 3.1. Roles of the ROI Leader

• Technical expert	• Cheerleader
• Consultant	• Communicator
• Problem solver	• Process monitor
• Initiator	• Planner
• Designer	• Analyst
• Developer	• Interpreter
• Coordinator	• Teacher

Exhibit 3.2. Skill Set for ROI Certification

- Planning for ROI calculations
- Collecting evaluation data
- Isolating the effects of programs
- Converting data to monetary values
- Monitoring program costs
- Analyzing data, including calculating the ROI
- Presenting evaluation data
- Implementing the ROI Methodology
- Providing internal consulting on the ROI Methodology
- Teaching others about the ROI Methodology

only a few programs to build these skills have been available. Now, many are available, and some are comprehensive. For example, the ROI Institute has developed a program to certify individuals who are assuming a leadership role in the implementation of the ROI Methodology. The process involves preliminary work and preparation prior to attending a one-week workshop. The week-long comprehensive workshop is the shortest of three ways to become certified in the ROI Methodology. All certification programs are designed to build essential skills needed to apply and implement the ROI process. Exhibit 3.2 lists the skills that are covered.

During the workshop, each participant plans a project for ROI evaluation, develops the data collection and ROI analysis plans for the project, and presents it to the other workshop participants for feedback. In addition, the participants develop and present plans to show how they will help implement the ROI Methodology in their organization, addressing the issues under their control. The typical participant is charged with implementing the ROI Methodology (or a part of it) in his or her division or organization. Sometimes, participants are part of an entire team that attends the certification workshop.

A public version of this certification workshop was first offered in 1995, when it became apparent that many organizations did not have the resources to send an entire team to an internal certification workshop but wanted instead to send one or two individuals to this type of session to develop the skills to lead the implementation of the ROI Methodology.

To date, more than 5,000 individuals, representing 3,000 organizations in fifty countries, have attended a certification workshop. Exhibit 3.3 shows a small sample of the private sector organizations that have participated in certification. Almost one-third of this group had an internal team certified. Others sent one or more individuals to a public workshop. Adoption of this strategy has been widespread; certification workshops have been conducted on every continent except Antarctica. No other process is available to satisfy this critical need; thus both internal and public certification are still very popular and successful. For more information on certification in the ROI Methodology, visit www.roiinstitute.net.

Apart from private sector organizations, many public sector organizations, including universities, nonprofit organizations, and health care providers, have participated in ROI certification. The organizations listed in Exhibit 3.4 represent a small sample of the many public sector organizations that have attended certification workshops.

Assigning Responsibilities

Determining specific responsibilities for implementation is a critical issue, because confusion arises when individuals are unclear about their specific assignments when implementing the ROI Methodology. Responsibilities apply to two broad groups. The first assignment is the entire program staff's responsibility for measurement and evaluation. All who are involved in designing, developing, delivering, coordinating, and supporting programs have some responsibility for measurement and evaluation. These responsibilities may include providing input on the design of instruments, planning a specific

Exhibit 3.3. Private Sector Organizations That Have Participated in Certification Workshops in the ROI Methodology

- Accenture
- Aetna
- Allstate Insurance Company
- Amazon.com
- AmSouth Bank
- Apple Computer
- Asia Pacific Breweries
- AT&T
- Bank of America
- BlueCross BlueShield
- Boston Scientific
- BP Amoco
- Bristol-Myers Squibb
- British Telecom
- Caltex Pacific
- Canadian Imperial Bank of Commerce
- Canadian Tire
- Chevron/Texaco
- CIGNA
- Cisco
- Comcast
- Commonwealth Edison
- CVS
- Delta Airlines
- Deloitte & Touche
- DHL Worldwide Express
- Discover Card
- Duke Energy
- Eli Lilly
- Eskom (South Africa)
- Federal Express
- First American Bank
- Ford Motor Company
- Genentech
- General Mills
- Georgia Pacific
- GlaxoSmithKline
- Harley Davidson
- Hewlett-Packard
- Hilton Hotels
- Hong Kong Bank
- HSBC
- IBM
- Intel
- Illinois Power
- KPMG
- Lockheed Martin
- M&M Mars
- MasterCard
- Mead
- Merck
- Meridian Hotels
- Microsoft
- Molson Coors
- Motorola
- NCR
- Nortel Networks
- Novus Services
- Olive Garden Restaurants
- Oversea-Chinese Banking Corporation
- Pfizer
- PriceWaterhouseCoopers
- Raytheon
- Rolls Royce
- SABMiller
- Scotia Bank

(Continued)

Exhibit 3.3. Private Sector Organizations That Have Participated in Certification Workshops in the ROI Methodology (*Continued*)

• Singapore Airlines	• Vodafone
• Singapore Technologies	• Volvo of North America
• Sprint/Nextel	• Wachovia Bank
• TD Canada Trust	• Wal-Mart
• Time Warner	• Waste Management Company
• United Parcel Service	• Wells Fargo
• UNOCAL	• Whirlpool
• Verizon Communications	• Xerox

evaluation, collecting data, or interpreting the results of a program. Typical responsibilities include these:

- Ensuring that the needs assessment addresses specific business impact measures targeted for improvement

- Developing application objectives (Level 3) and business impact objectives (Level 4) for each program

- Focusing the content of the program on performance improvement, ensuring that exercises, tests, case studies, and skill practices relate to the desired objectives

- Keeping participants focused on application and impact objectives

- Communicating the rationale and reasons for evaluation

- Assisting with follow-up activities to capture application and business impact data

- Providing assistance with data collection, data analysis, and reporting

- Developing plans for data collection and analysis

Exhibit 3.4. Public Sector Organizations That Have Participated in Certification Workshops in the ROI Methodology

Federal Government

Department of Defense, Department of Homeland Security, Department of Labor, Department of the Treasury, Department of Veterans Affairs, Office of Personnel Management

State Government

California, Colorado, Mississippi, Washington

Higher Education

Harvard University, Indiana University, Lansing Community College, Penn State University, University of Southern Mississippi

Healthcare

Banner Healthcare, Baptist Health Systems, Children's Hospitals, Covenant Healthcare System, Guthrie Healthcare, Los Angeles Hospital

- Presenting evaluation data to target audiences

- Assisting with the design of instruments

While having each member of the staff involved in all of these activities may be appropriate, each individual should have one or more of these responsibilities as part of their routine job duties. This assignment of responsibility keeps the implementation of the ROI Methodology from being disjointed and separate from major organizational activities. More important, it allocates accountability to those who develop, deliver, and implement the programs.

The second assignment of responsibility involves technical support. Those responsible for technical support are usually the ROI champions and ROI leaders. If the department and its staff are large, it may be helpful to establish a group of technical experts to assist in implementing the ROI Methodology. When this group is established, everyone must understand that these experts are provided not to relieve others of evaluation responsibilities but to supplement their technical expertise. For example, at one time, Accenture had a full-time measurement and evaluation staff of thirty-two individuals to provide technical support for the evaluation of internal professional education. Today, because program staff capabilities have been developed so that individuals can share evaluation responsibilities, full-time staff number less than ten, even though there are now more programs and more employees.

When technical support is developed, responsibilities center on eight key areas:

1. Designing data collection instruments

2. Assisting with development of an evaluation strategy

3. Coordinating a major evaluation project

4. Analyzing data, including specialized statistical analyses

5. Interpreting results and making specific recommendations

6. Developing an evaluation report or case study to communicate overall results

7. Presenting results to critical audiences

8. Providing technical support in any phase of the ROI Methodology

Assignment of responsibilities for evaluation is an issue that may require attention throughout the process. Although the entire staff must have specific responsibilities, others in support functions may need to be responsible for data collection. These responsibilities are defined when a particular evaluation strategy plan is developed and approved.

Tapping into a Network

Because the ROI Methodology is new to many individuals, having a peer group of individuals who are experiencing similar issues and frustrations can be helpful. Tapping into an international network that is already developed, joining or creating a local network, or building an internal network are all ways to access the resources, ideas, and support of others.

The ROI Network

In 1996, the ROI Network was created to facilitate the exchange of information among the graduates of the ROI Certification™ workshop. During the certification process, the participants bond and freely exchange information with each other. The ROI Network provides a permanent vehicle for information and support.

The ROI Network, which claims about 4,000 members, is supported by the ROI Institute, Inc. The network operates through a variety of committees and communicates with members through newsletters, Web sites, list serves, and annual meetings. The ROI Network represents an opportunity to build a community of practice around the ROI Methodology. To learn more about the ROI Network, visit www.roiinstitute.net.

Local Networks

In some situations, establishing a group of local individuals who share similar interests in and concerns about the ROI Methodology may be feasible. A local network can be set up in a country (for example, the Irish ROI Network) or in a more confined entity (for example, the Puerto Rico ROI Network). In Puerto Rico, a group of one hundred individuals who participated in the certification process challenged each other to remain together as a group in order to discuss issues and report progress. Members come from a wide variety of backgrounds, and they meet routinely to report progress; discuss problems, barriers, and issues; and plan next steps. This active group is typical of what can develop if individuals are willing to share information and support each other. Sometimes, a statewide network, such as the California ROI Network, is created. In a few cases, a citywide network, such as the Toronto ROI Network, has been created.

Internal Networks

One way to integrate the needs of practitioners for an effective ROI evaluation process is through an internal ROI network.

Organizations in which networks have been created report that they are powerful tools for accelerating skill development in evaluation, as well as for cultivating a new culture of accountability.

The concept of an internal network is simple. The idea is to bring together people from throughout an organization who are interested in ROI evaluations to work under the guidance of trained ROI evaluators. Typically, advocates for the network within a function or department see both the need for beginning a network and the potential of ROI evaluation to change how the function does its work. Interested network members learn by designing and executing real evaluation plans. This process generates commitment for accountability as a new way of doing business.

Developing Evaluation Targets for the Staff

ROI Fundamentals, the first book in this series, explains that establishing targets for evaluation levels is an important way to make progress in measurement and evaluation. Targets enable the staff to focus on improvements at specific evaluation levels. The percentage of programs to be evaluated at each level must be targeted.

The first step in developing targets is to assess the current situation. The number of programs, including repeated sessions of a program, is tabulated, along with the level (or levels) of evaluation conducted for each program. Next, the percentage of programs collecting Level 1 (Reaction) data is calculated or estimated. This process is repeated for each level of evaluation. The initial percentages for evaluations at Levels 3, 4, and 5 are usually low.

After determining the current situation, the next step is to establish a realistic target for each level within a specific time frame. Many organizations set annual targets for the percentages. This process should involve input from the entire program team to ensure that the targets are realistic and that the staff is committed to the process and the targets. If the staff does not develop ownership of this process, the targets will not be met. The targets must be achievable yet challenging and motivating. Table 3.1 shows the

Table 3.1. Evaluation Targets for a Large Pharmaceutical Company

Level of Evaluation	Percentage of Programs Evaluated at this Level
Level 0: Inputs and Indicators	100%
Level 1: Reaction	100
Level 2: Learning	70
Level 3: Application	30
Level 4: Business Impact	10
Level 5: ROI	5

targets for a large pharmaceutical company with hundreds of programs.

In the pharmaceutical company described in Table 3.1, 100 percent of the programs are to be measured at Levels 0 and 1, which is consistent with many other organizations. Seventy percent of the programs will be measured at Level 2, using a formal method of measurement. At Level 3, 30 percent of the programs will collect application data. This means that almost one-third of the programs will have some type of follow-up method, at least for a small sample of participants. Ten percent of programs are planned for business impact evaluations, and half of those will have ROI evaluations. These percentages are typical and are often recommended, although the Level 2 percentage may increase significantly if formal testing or informal measures (such as self-assessments) are used to evaluate learning. In many companies, there is no need to go beyond 10 percent and 5 percent at Level 4 and Level 5, respectively.

Table 3.2 shows the current percentages (year 0) and the targets for four years in a large Eastern European multinational company. This table reflects the gradual improvement of increasing evaluation activity at Levels 3, 4, and 5. In this firm, several issues involving infrastructure and organizational culture had to be addressed before major performance improvement could be expected.

Table 3.2. Percentage Targets for Four Years in a Large Eastern European Company

	Percentage of Programs Evaluated				
	Year 0	Year 1	Year 2	Year 3	Year 4
Level 0: Inputs and Indicators	85%	90%	95%	100%	100%
Level 1: Reaction and Planned Action	74	85	95	100	100
Level 2: Learning	32	40	50	60	65
Level 3: Application	0	10	15	20	25
Level 4: Business Impact	0	2	4	6	10
Level 5: ROI	0	1	2	4	5

Target setting is a critical implementation issue. It should be completed early in the process, with the full support of the entire program staff. Also, if it is practical and feasible, the targets should have the approval of key managers, particularly the senior management team.

Preparing the Program Staff

One group that will often resist implementation of the ROI Methodology is the staff that must design, develop, deliver, and coordinate the programs. These staff members often see evaluation as an unnecessary intrusion on their responsibilities that will absorb precious time and stifle their freedom to be creative. This section outlines some important issues that must be addressed when preparing staff for implementing the ROI Methodology.

Involving the Staff

The program staff should be involved in the process whenever a key issue is being resolved or a major decision is being made. As policy statements are prepared and evaluation guidelines are developed, staff input is essential. It is difficult for staff members to be critical of something that they helped design, develop, and plan. Using meetings, brainstorming sessions, and task forces, staff should be involved in every phase of developing the framework and the supporting documents for implementing the ROI Methodology. Ideally, staff would learn the process in a two-day workshop and, at the same time, develop guidelines, policies, and application targets. This approach is efficient, allowing participants to complete several key tasks at the same time.

Using ROI as a Learning Tool

Many reasons for staff resistance to implementation of the ROI Methodology have been discussed in this book. One of those reasons is that the effectiveness of their programs that are being evaluated will be fully exposed, placing their reputation on the line. Some participants may have a fear of failure. To overcome this fear, the ROI Methodology should be clearly positioned as a tool for process improvement and not a tool to evaluate staff performance, at least during the early years of its implementation. Staff members will not be interested in developing a tool that will be used to expose their shortcomings and failures.

Evaluators can actually learn more from failures than from successes. If a program is not working, it is best to find out quickly and to gain insight into critical issues firsthand rather than to find out from others. If a program is ineffective and not producing the desired results, that fact will eventually be known to clients or the management team, if they are not already aware of it. A lack of results will cause managers to become less supportive of programs. Dwindling support takes many forms, ranging from budget reductions to refusing to let individuals participate in programs. If the weaknesses of programs are identified and adjustments are made quickly, not only will more effective programs be developed and promoted but the credibility of the function or department and the respect for its staff will increase.

Addressing Objections to Implementation

Several objections to the implementation of the ROI Methodology will usually be encountered. Some of these reflect real barriers, while others are based on misconceptions. Most of these were presented and analyzed in the preceding chapter. However, the most common objections from the staff and ways to address them are reviewed here.

- *ROI is a complex process.* Many members of the program staff will perceive the ROI Methodology as too complex to implement. To counter this perception, the staff must be shown how the process can be simplified by breaking it into manageable components and steps. Many tools, templates, and software programs that simplify the use of the ROI Methodology are available. (The Appendix of *ROI Fundamentals*, the first book in this series, lists many of these tools.)

- *We have no time for evaluation.* Staff members need to understand that evaluation can save time in the future. An ROI impact study may show that a program should be slightly modified, radically changed, or even eliminated, thereby improving their processes, which results in efficiency gains. Thoroughly planning the evaluation strategy can save additional follow-up time.

- *Management does not require evaluation.* Most staff members know when top managers are pushing the accountability issue. If they do not see that push, they may be reluctant to take the time to make the ROI Methodology work. They must be helped to see the benefits of pursuing the process, even if it is not required or encouraged from the top. The staff should see the ROI Methodology as a preventive strategy or leading-edge strategy. The payoff of implementation should be underscored.

- *Results will lead to criticism.* Many staff members will be concerned about how the results of ROI impact studies will be used. If the results are used to criticize or evaluate the performance of program designers or facilitators, they will be reluctant to embrace the concept. The ROI Methodology should be considered a learning process.

These and other objections can thwart an otherwise successful implementation. Each must be addressed or reduced to a manageable issue.

Teaching the Staff

The program staff may have inadequate skills in measurement and evaluation in general and in the ROI Methodology specifically and thus may need to develop some expertise. Measurement and evaluation is not always a formal part of preparing to become a facilitator, designer, performance analyst, or program leader. Therefore, each staff member must be provided with training on how to implement the ROI Methodology step by step. In addition, staff members must learn how to develop plans for collecting and analyzing data and how to interpret the results of data analysis. A one- or two-day workshop can be used to build their skills and knowledge and can enable them to understand the ROI Methodology, appreciate what it can accomplish for the organization, understand its necessity, and participate in a successful implementation. (A list of public two-day workshops is available at www.roiintitute.net. Teaching materials, outlines, slides, workbooks, and other support materials for workshops are also available through the ROI Institute.) Each staff member should understand the ROI Methodology and should know how to utilize and support it.

ROI Evaluations

The first tangible evidence of success with the ROI Methodology may be initiation of the first program for which the ROI is calculated. This section outlines some key issues involved in identifying the programs that are appropriate for ROI evaluations and keeping them on track.

Selecting Programs for ROI Evaluation

Selecting a program for ROI analysis is an important issue. Under most circumstances, certain types of programs are more suitable for comprehensive, detailed analyses. *ROI Fundamentals*, the first book of this series, briefly explains that typically, the programs identified as appropriate for ROI evaluation are expensive, strategic, and highly visible. Exhibit 3.5 lists six common criteria used to select programs for this level of evaluation. The process for selection is simple. Using a list like the one in Exhibit 3.5 or a more detailed one, each program is rated on each criterion. A typical scale uses ratings of 1 to 5. All programs are rated, and the program with the highest number is the best candidate for ROI evaluation. This process only identifies the best candidates. Which programs are actually evaluated may depend on other factors, such as the resources available to conduct the studies.

Additional criteria should be considered when selecting the first programs for ROI evaluations. For example, the first program should be as simple as possible. Complex programs should be evaluated later, after ROI evaluation skills have been mastered. Also, the initial program should be one that is currently considered successful. (For example, all the current feedback data suggest that the program adds significant value.) This criterion helps avoid a negative ROI on the first use of the ROI Methodology. Still another criterion is that the program be free of strong political issues or biases. While such programs can be effectively evaluated with the ROI Methodology, it is better to avoid the complexity that may be added by controversy in early applications.

Exhibit 3.5. Selection Tool for ROI Evaluations

Criteria	Programs				
	#1	#2	#3	#4	#5
1. Life cycle					
2. Company objectives					
3. Costs					
4. Audience size					
5. Visibility					
6. Management interest					
Total					

Rating Scale	
1. Life cycle	1 = short life cycle
	5 = long life cycle
2. Company objectives	1 = not directly related to company objectives
	5 = closely related to company objectives
3. Costs	1 = inexpensive
	5 = expensive
4. Audience size	1 = small audience
	5 = large audience
5. Visibility	1 = low visibility
	5 = high visibility
6. Management interest	1 = low level of interest in evaluation
	5 = high level of interest in evaluation

We have touched on only the basic criteria; criteria can be added as needed to bring the organization's evaluation issues into focus. Some large organizations with hundreds of programs in a corporate university use as many as fifteen criteria to determine which programs should be targeted for ROI evaluation. The most important point is to select the programs that are designed to make a difference and represent tremendous investments by the organization. Also, programs that command much attention from senior management are ideal candidates for an ROI evaluation. Almost any senior management group will have a perception about the effectiveness of a particular program. Senior managers may definitely want to know the impact of some programs but be less concerned about others. Therefore, management interest may drive the selection of programs to be evaluated at Level 5 (ROI).

The next major step is to determine how many programs to evaluate initially and in which areas. Evaluating a small number of programs is recommended at first, perhaps two or three. The selected programs may represent the functional areas of the business, such as operations, sales, finance, engineering, and information systems. A similar approach is to select programs that represent different areas within a function; for example, within the organizational function of learning and development, programs such as sales training, management and supervisor training, computer-based training, and technical training might represent a sample of the various areas. It is important to select a manageable number so that the process will be implemented.

Ultimately, the number of programs selected will depend on the resources available to conduct the studies, as well as the internal need for higher levels of accountability. Evaluation of programs at the percentages indicated in Table 3.1 can be accomplished within 3 to 5 percent of the total learning and development budget. For a learning and development organization with two hundred programs, this would mean that in a given year, 5 percent (ten) of the programs would receive ROI evaluations and at least 30 percent (sixty programs) would receive some type of follow-up (Level 3) evaluation. The entire program can be accomplished for less than 5 percent of the total learning and development budget. The costs of the ROI Methodology need not drain the resources of an organization; nonetheless, the programs selected for Level 5 analysis should be limited and should be carefully selected.

Reporting Progress

When programs are developed and implementation of the ROI Methodology gets under way, status meetings should be conducted in order to report progress and discuss critical issues with appropriate team members. For example, if a leadership program is selected as one of the programs for ROI evaluation, all the key staff members involved in the program (design, development, and delivery) should meet regularly to discuss its status. This keeps the program team focused on the critical issues, generates the best ideas for addressing problems and barriers, and builds a knowledge base for evaluating future programs. Sometimes, this group is facilitated by an external consultant who is an expert in the ROI Methodology. In other cases, the internal ROI leader may facilitate the group.

These meetings serve three major purposes: reporting progress, learning, and planning. The meeting usually begins with a status report on each ROI program, describing what has been accomplished since the previous meeting. Next, specific barriers and problems are discussed. During the discussions, new issues may be interjected as the group considers possible tactics, techniques, or tools that can be used to remove barriers or solve problems. Finally, the group focuses on suggestions and recommendations for next steps, developing specific plans.

Preparing the Management Team

Perhaps no group is more important to successful implementation of the ROI Methodology than the management team responsible for allocating resources for programs and providing other kinds of support for them. In addition, the management team often provides valuable input and assistance for the implementation. Specific actions to train and develop the management team should be carefully planned and executed.

Building an Effective Partnership Between Program Staff and Senior Management

A critical issue that must be addressed in preparing the managers is the relationship between the program staff and key managers. A productive partnership is needed; each party must understand the concerns, problems, and opportunities of the other. Developing this type of relationship is a long-term process that must be deliberately planned and initiated by key staff members. The decision to commit resources and support for a program is often based on the effectiveness of this relationship.

Training Managers

One effective way to prepare managers for implementation of the ROI Methodology is to conduct a workshop on the "Manager's Role in Learning and Performance." Varying in duration from one-half to two days, this practical workshop shapes critical skills and changes perceptions to enhance the support of the ROI methodology. Managers leave the workshop with an improved perception of the impact of programs and a clearer understanding of their role in the implementation process. More important, managers often renew their commitment to making programs within their organization successful.

Target Audience

While the target audience for this workshop is usually middle-level managers, this may vary. In some organizations, the target may be senior managers, and in others, the target may be middle-level managers. Three important questions will help determine the proper audience:

- Which group has the most direct influence on the programs being implemented?

- Which management group is causing serious problems through a lack of support?

- Which group needs to understand the ROI Methodology so that group members can influence the implementation of programs and the methodology?

The answer to these questions is often "middle-level managers."

Timing

This workshop should be conducted early in the management development process, before nonsupportive habits are developed. When the ROI Methodology is implemented throughout the organization, it is best to educate high-level managers first and then work down the organization. If possible, a version of the workshop should become part of the traditional management development program required for supervisors when they are promoted into managerial positions.

Enlisting Support from Top Management

Convincing top management to require this workshop may be difficult; at least three approaches can be taken:

1. Discuss and illustrate the consequences of inadequate management support for programs and evaluation. For example, the statistics on wasted time and money when the programming process does not work are staggering.

2. Show how current support is lacking. An evaluation of a program will often reveal the barriers to successful application and implementation. Lack of management support is often the main reason, a fact that brings the issue close to home and illustrates the importance of this support.

3. Demonstrate how money can be saved and how results can be achieved by using the ROI Methodology.

Endorsement of the top management group is important. In some organizations, top managers actually attend the workshop in order to explore firsthand what is involved and what they must do to make the process work. At a minimum, top management should support the program by signing memos describing the program or by approving policy statements about the content of the workshop. They should also ask provocative questions about evaluation in their staff meetings from time to time. This will not happen by chance; executives may need tactful coaching.

Content

The program will usually cover the topics outlined in this section. The program can be developed in separate modules, and managers can be exempted from some modules based on their previous knowledge or experience with the topic. Using the module concept is recommended.

The Overall Importance of Programs. Managers need to be convinced that programs are a mainstream responsibility that is gaining importance and influence in many organizations. They need to understand the results-based approach of progressive functions or departments. After completing this module, managers should perceive programs and projects as critical processes in their organization and should be able to describe how programs contribute to strategic and operational objectives. Data from the organization should be presented to show the full scope of the function's impact within the organization. Tangible evidence of top management commitment to the ROI Methodology should be presented in the form of memos, directives, or policies signed by the CEO or another appropriate top executive. In some organizations, the invitation to attend the workshop comes from the CEO, a gesture that shows strong commitment from top management. Also, external data should be included to illustrate the growth of the unit's budget and the increasing importance of the unit's programs within the organization. Presenting a case study that shows the link between specific programs and the organization's overall strategy might be helpful.

The Impact of Programs. Too often, managers are unsure whether programs have been successful or useful. After completing this module, managers will be able to identify the steps for measuring the impact of specific types of programs on important output measures. Reports and studies that show the impact of programs, using measures such as productivity, quality, cost, response times, and customer satisfaction, should be presented. Internal evaluation reports, if available, should be presented to managers, showing convincing evidence that a variety of programs make a significant difference within the organization. If internal reports are not available, other success stories or case studies from other organizations can be used. Managers need to be convinced that their unit's programs, whatever the function or department, are successful and results-based, not only to help effect change but also to meet critical organizational goals and objectives.

The Process of Program Development and Evaluation. Managers usually will not support activities or processes that they do not fully understand. After completing this module, managers should be able to describe how the program development and evaluation process works within the organization and understand each critical step, from needs assessment to ROI calculation. Managers need to be aware of the effort that goes into developing and evaluating a program and their role in each step of the process. Presenting a short case study that illustrates all the steps is helpful. This discussion also reveals different areas of the potential impact of programs.

Responsibilities During the Process. Defining who is responsible for programs is important to their success. After completing this module, managers should be able to list their specific responsibilities for successful programs. Managers must see how they can influence programs and the degree of responsibility they must assume in the future. Multilevel responsibility for programs is advocated—that is, managers, participants, participants' managers, trainers, developers, and facilitators should share the responsibility. Case studies should be presented that illustrate the consequences when responsibilities are neglected or when managers fail to follow up. In some organizations, job descriptions are revised to reflect these responsibilities. In other organizations, major job-related goals are established in order to highlight management responsibility for programs. Overall, this module should leave the participants with a clear understanding of how their responsibilities are linked to the success of any program within the organization.

Active Involvement. One of the most important ways to increase manager support is to get managers actively involved in a process. After completing this module, managers will often commit to one or more avenues of active involvement in the future. Exhibit 3.6 shows twelve avenues for management involvement that were identified in one company. The information in the exhibit was presented to managers during the workshop with a request for them to commit to at least one area of involvement. After these areas were fully explained and discussed, each manager was asked to select one or more ways in which he or she would become involved in program development and evaluation in the future.

Exhibit 3.6. Management Involvement in Learning and Development

Following are twelve areas for present and future involvement in the learning and development process. Please check your areas of planned involvement.

	Within Your Area	Outside Your Area
• Attend a program designed for your staff	☐	☐
• Provide input on a needs analysis	☐	☐
• Serve on an advisory committee	☐	☐
• Provide input on program design	☐	☐
• Serve as a subject matter expert	☐	☐
• Serve on a task force to develop a program	☐	☐
• Volunteer to evaluate an external learning and development program	☐	☐
• Assist in the selection of a vendor-supplied learning and development program	☐	☐
• Provide reinforcement to your employees after they attend a program	☐	☐
• Coordinate a program	☐	☐
• Assist in program evaluation or follow-up	☐	☐
• Conduct a portion of the program as a facilitator	☐	☐

A commitment to sign up for at least one involvement role was required.

If used properly, these commitments can be a rich source of input and assistance from the management group. There will be many offers for involvement, and the function or department must follow through. A quick follow-up on all offers is recommended.

Monitoring Progress and Communicating Results

The final part of the implementation process is to monitor the overall progress made and communicate the results of programs selected for ROI evaluations. Although it is often an overlooked part of the process, an effective communication plan can help keep implementation on target and let others know how the use of the ROI Methodology is affecting an organization.

Communication must be an ongoing part of the process in order to ensure that all stakeholders know their responsibilities, understand the progress made and barriers confronted, and develop insight into the results and successes achieved. Because communication is so important in the ROI Methodology, this topic was explored in Chapter One, which provides comprehensive coverage of all the issues involved in communicating the results of programs and providing routine feedback for decision making and process improvement. Detailed information on how to develop and present an impact study is also included in that chapter.

Final Thoughts

Building capability in the ROI Methodology and support for its use is a critical part of implementation. If it is not approached in a systematic, logical way, the ROI Methodology will not become an integral part of the development and evaluation of programs and projects, and accountability for programs will be lacking. This chapter presents the elements that must be considered and the issues that must be addressed in order to ensure that capability and support are established and that implementation is as smooth as possible. The result should be full integration of the ROI Methodology as a mainstream activity in the program evaluation process.

4

Sustaining the Use of the ROI Methodology

Keeping the Process on Track

K eeping the process on track is one of the biggest challenges of ROI Methodology implementation. Staying on track in the face of continual change and maintaining the health and integrity of the process over time typically pose formidable challenges to an organization's efforts to create enduring, systemwide results-based measurement and evaluation.

This chapter explores the stages of implementation and identifies the inhibitors and enablers of successful integration of the ROI Methodology and outlines the strategies for facilitating integration of the ROI Methodology over time.

As in any change effort, consistent attention and focus must be maintained in order to build and sustain the evaluation process. Chapter Three examined the importance of building internal capabilities and skill sets in order to help develop and maintain a results-based measurement and evaluation process. Without this attention, the organization's commitment to the ROI Methodology might wane and the process might be labeled another "flavor of the month." Long-term, effective evaluation solutions must stand the test of time. Emphasizing the ROI Methodology as a long-term process improvement tool adds value and keeps it from becoming a passing fad or a short-term phenomenon.

Motivation for long-term implementation could come initially from the results of a current impact study. Motivation may also be maintained as programs continue to be adjusted, modified, enhanced, or eliminated to add value. To ensure complete integration of the ROI Methodology as a mainstream approach, critical stages in implementation must be addressed. This final chapter will help you to anticipate the predictable stages of implementation, identify signs and symptoms of implementation trouble spots that may require action, and move past trouble spots by taking actions to remain on track.

The Challenges of Sustainability

Why might implementation of the ROI Methodology fail to be sustained in an organization? Here are the top reasons, which occur in all types of business environments.

- Lack of a clear vision or goal

- Changing directions in midstream

- Conflicting priorities

- Inadequate communication

- Unmet customer expectations

- No buy-in or support from key stakeholders

- Ineffective leadership

- Inadequate planning or no planning

- No clear understanding of what needs to be done (who is going to do what by when)

- Change in scope

- Not enough resources

- Unrealistic expectations

Each of these issues must be addressed in both short-term and long-term implementation. In the short term, applying tips, tools, and strategies from Chapter Two will help mitigate many of these issues. High-level strategies for addressing each challenge are shown in Table 4.1.

It may be helpful to identify which implementation issues have posed or may pose the greatest threat to the success of the impact study. The tactics and tools to address the issues should then be identified, and action plans should be put in place to prevent problems. To add context in regard to the appropriate time and place for use of these methods for addressing implementation issues, it is important to understand the typical stages in implementation of the ROI Methodology.

Stages of Implementation

As the ROI Methodology is introduced and integrated into a workplace, predictable obstacles to progress often arise. Large or small, public or private, most organizations undergo distinct stages on their journey toward increased accountability. As Figure 4.1 shows, these stages are part of a naturally evolving process.

Stage 1: Recognition

In the recognition stage, an organization realizes that accountability for evaluation is an issue, and preliminary action is taken. This stage is usually initiated by a single person or a small group, and at this point, implementation of the ROI Methodology is not viewed as a strategic imperative by senior management. For these reasons, commitment may be limited or marginal, and long-lasting evaluation processes are not yet in place. Indicators of the recognition stage are noted as readiness issues in the assessment "Is Your Organization a Candidate for Implementation of the

Table 4.1. Causes of Ineffective Implementation

If Your Organization Is Experiencing . . .	Then . . .	Support Tools
Lack of a clear vision or goal	Initiate goal setting, stakeholder communication, and action planning based on the value of a results-based measurement focus.	Communication briefings Communication plan
Changing directions midstream	Integrate change efforts into existing management systems and cycles such as • Business planning • Budget development • Corporate and departmental measurement plans • Compensation planning • Succession planning	Implementation issues to address with your sponsor
Conflicting priorities	Balance organizational priorities to protect resources dedicated to ROI implementation efforts. Make necessary compromises or adjustments in the implementation schedule in order to meet organizational needs.	Transition plan Project plan

Inadequate communication	Commit to regular review meetings to assess progress. Make performance data available to implementation team members or stakeholders.	Communication plan Transfer strategy matrix Action planning
Unmet customer expectations	Develop metrics and communication methods in order to routinely track progress and productivity.	Stakeholder identification
No buy-in or support from key stakeholders	Meet with key stakeholders from client organizations to define the value proposition of a results-based measurement focus.	Stakeholder identification Stakeholder engagement Management involvement checklist Communication briefings
Ineffective leadership	Solicit a credible sponsor. Use a credible, competent evaluation lead. Follow up on established consequences if desired performance levels are not being achieved. Identify tactics to build program team strengths and minimize weaknesses.	Professional development, training, or ROI certification for internal staff Senior or mid-level management briefings Best-practice benchmarking Professional networking
Inadequate planning or no planning	Work from an implementation plan. Initiate a task force to address and remove inhibitors.	Project plan Transition plan Data collection plan Roles and responsibilities matrix Evaluation team charter Transfer strategy matrix

(Continued)

Table 4.1. Causes of Ineffective Implementation (*Continued*)

If Your Organization Is Experiencing . . .	Then . . .	Support Tools
No clear understanding of what needs to be done (who is going to do what by when)	Plan and deploy well. Break down implementation tasks into manageable, meaningful activities. Ensure adequate staffing and funding to support the implementation plan.	Project plan Transition plan Data collection plan Roles and responsibilities matrix Evaluation team charter Transfer strategy matrix
Change in scope	Communicate implementation plan, scope, schedule, and resource requirements to appropriate executives or stakeholders.	Project plan Transition plan Data collection plan Roles and responsibilities matrix Transfer strategy matrix
Not enough resources	Acknowledge legitimate organizational issues of capacity and resource constraints. Use cost-saving approaches to consolidate steps and conserve resources. Conduct ROI impact studies on a selective basis.	Ten cost-saving approaches Selection criteria matrix
Unrealistic expectations	Continually ensure that results are related to business and strategic goals. Address organizational myths, fears, and concerns.	Matching objectives with needs Stakeholder identification Communication plan Myths, fears, and countermeasures worksheet

Figure 4.1. Stages in Implementation of the ROI Methodology

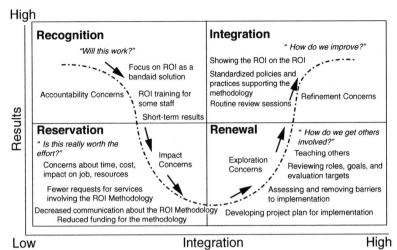

Source: Adapted from Scott and Jaffe, 1999.

ROI Methodology?" in Chapter Two. These issues include such factors as:

- Expenditures of a department or function are identified as significant.

- An organization is undergoing important change.

- Complaints or concerns from clients about the value of programs and services have been noted.

- A department or function has a history of more than one program disaster.

- Clients or decision makers are demanding that the department or function show bottom-line results.

- The focus on linking the department or function to strategic directions of the organization has increased.

- The department or function has a low investment in measurement and evaluation.

- The department or function is a key player in current change initiatives.

- The unit competes with other departments or functions for resources.

- The department's or function's image is less than satisfactory.

The responsibility of a program team at this stage is finding solutions. Some of the necessary tasks at the recognition stage are as follows:

1. Remove barriers to implementation and facilitate problem solving by taking some of the following actions:
   - Make sure that the program team or ROI champion is an effective change agent.
   - Assess the needs of the organization.
   - Establish partnerships between the program team and key stakeholders.
   - Obtain executive input.
   - Prepare your organization for the changes that will occur as it shifts to a results-based focus.

2. Initiate goal setting, stakeholder communication, and action planning to show the value of a results-based measurement focus. Complete these actions:
   - Relate the change effort to organizational strategies.
   - Identify and research the factors that will affect change strategies within your organization.
   - Plan, communicate, and deploy all programs effectively.

- Consistently educate executives and senior management on the requirements for implementing the ROI Methodology so that funding and staffing will be adequate.
- Ensure that time and resources are available for the evaluation team to develop the skills required for proper implementation.
- Make sure that the program team is aware of any resource constraints within the organization.

3. Initiate short-term solutions:
   - Select, orient, and educate program team members about what is required for implementation of the ROI Methodology.
   - Institute a reward system that is linked to desired program outcomes, and communicate it to all parties prior to implementation.
   - Identify one to three "quick hit" opportunities, and use them to show the value of the ROI Methodology.

4. Evaluate solutions in order to determine whether they meet organizational goals. Use these methods to:
   - Hold weekly review meetings in order to assess implementation progress.
   - Assign responsibilities for deliverables.
   - Define metrics for tracking progress and productivity.

Stage 2: Reservation

In the reservation stage, symptoms that the ROI Methodology is no longer achieving its intended objectives may begin to emerge. For example, renewed objections may arise about the impact of the process on time and resources, or an organization may become preoccupied with new business demands that compete for time and resources. Stakeholders may become impatient and may voice the concern that the investment of time and effort needed to move toward a results-based focus is not worth it. The initial support and goodwill resulting from preliminary successes with the process may have waned. It is not uncommon at this stage for an organization to abandon the effort or to significantly decrease support from what was originally committed.

Indicators that an organization is in the reservation stage include these:

- Reduced funding for the process of ROI evaluation

- Fewer communications about the programs and processes

- Lack of participation and involvement of the management team

- Constant shuffling of people involved in the process

- Fewer requests for products and services related to the accountability process

- Postponing or eliminating review sessions aimed at keeping the process on track

- Complaints about the time or cost required for evaluation activities

- A change of direction toward some other process that appears to be competing with or eliminating the need for the accountability

- Reduction in the dissemination of information and communication on the progress of the ROI Methodology and ROI studies, even in a streamlined fashion

Several key tasks are required at the reservation stage.

1. The program leader or ROI champion must jump-start individuals and groups and eliminate inertia by doing the following:

   - Break implementation and program tasks into manageable, meaningful activities.

   - Develop contingency plans to bolster participants in the implementation (including program team members) who may have become worn down by the process.

   - An implementation plan should have been developed prior to implementation. Rigorously adhere to this plan, and make sure all participants have a copy of it.

   - Encourage program team members to contribute information and insights on how to revive the implementation effort.

   - Ensure that the results sought from implementation are manageable in the time frame allowed.

2. Initial goal setting and action planning should be reactivated by doing the following:

   - Translate the details of the change effort into job-level details and tasks, then assign them to implementation team members, who will be responsible and accountable for carrying them out.

   - Ask participants' managers to link performance appraisals with individual accomplishments related to implementation of the ROI Methodology, if appropriate.

   - Identify the budget impacts of implementation efforts.

   - Hold regular meetings in order to inform executives and stakeholders about the status of implementation and to gather input.

   - Get financial experts involved in estimating the financial impact of the change on your organization.

3. Enthusiasm about the desired future state should be rejuvenated through performing these tasks:

    - Share with all the success of those who have implemented the ROI Methodology.

    - If some metrics are not improving as projected, identify more appropriate metrics with which to measure progress.

    - Try holding a contest in order to address an issue involved in the results-based change effort.

    - Continually assess the implementation process and conditions, and change them as necessary to ensure success.

    - Publicize and celebrate successes and progress toward goals.

    - Avoid bragging and boasting about success, even if some progress is being made.

4. Objections to the process should be openly addressed with these actions:

    - Initiate a task force to address and remove inhibitors to the process, and use the influence of management or other stakeholders to neutralize problems or remove obstacles.

    - Discount any negative rumors, and reconfigure systems or dynamics that could foster negativity.

    - Have the implementation team follow up relentlessly with stakeholders.

    - Report apprehensions about the implementation plan, scope, or schedule to executives or stakeholders.

    - Establish clear milestones for the implementation plan.

5. Consistent messages about the vision and purpose of the implementation and the value of change should be repeated to the stakeholders. Try these ideas:

- Leverage personal alliances to communicate business drivers for the change effort.
- Assign the executive sponsor and key stakeholders specific accountabilities and responsibilities.
- Set an example by seizing learning opportunities, and communicate about them on a regular basis.
- Develop a communication plan and follow it.

Stage 3: Renewal

In the renewal stage, an organization starts to move past its inhibitors and explores how to renew its initial commitment to invest in expanded evaluation solutions. The need for integrated evaluation processes and solutions achieves increased visibility and attention from internal staff, including senior management. Some of the indicators that an organization or function is in the renewal stage include the following:

- Adjustments in the evaluation process and organizational course corrections toward the desired state are initiated.

- The ROI Methodology, its concepts, and its value are embraced.

- Mechanisms for monitoring and addressing mindsets, behaviors, and practices in regard to evaluation are renewed.

- Energy and potential chaos increase as team members identify where further support is needed and consider how to get it.

- Some conflict arises as multiple solutions are explored.

Several key tasks need to be performed at the renewal stage.

1. Recognize and define needs within the change process at each leverage point by doing the following:
   - Continue to monitor milestone achievements, needs, and gaps.
   - Scale back plans, if necessary.
   - Integrate change efforts into existing management systems and cycles, such as
     - Business planning
     - Budget development
     - Corporate and departmental measurement planning
     - Compensation planning
     - Succession planning
     - Employee orientation and training
   - Link accomplishments in ROI evaluation to individual performance appraisals, include accomplishment of goals as a criterion in team bonus plans, and give informal rewards—such as congratulatory notes or special luncheons—to participants in the implementation.
   - Have the implementation team continually ensure that results are related to business and strategic goals.
   - Tailor targets and metrics to the appropriate organizational life cycles.

2. Encourage teamwork and interdependence with these actions:
   - Incorporate action-oriented program members into the implementation effort.
   - Continually monitor the effectiveness of the implementation team.
   - Identify the program team's strengths, and minimize its weaknesses.
   - Close any skill gaps in special ROI training.

- Develop a charter for the team that is implementing the ROI Methodology.
- Avoid changes in the implementation team.
- Address issues involving the implementation team immediately; do not let issues fester unchecked.

3. Keep the implementation team focused on priorities and short-term goals with these actions:

  - Keep the program and metrics simple.
  - Agree on data sources; clearly define the source of each metric, who should obtain the information, and how the information will be reported.
  - Incorporate a review of performance data into routine implementation meetings, and make it available to stakeholders prior to the meetings.

4. Recognize and reward small wins by doing the following:

  - Identify and communicate any examples of success that signify that the ROI Methodology and its implementation are taking hold within your organization. Routinely report this information to management.
  - Establish communication vehicles for informing all stakeholders of achievements in implementation. Address all milestones outlined in the communication plan, and communicate their status.
  - Present formal and informal rewards for efforts made in implementing the ROI Methodology; participants achieve the things for which they are rewarded.

Stage 4: Integration

In the integration stage, enabling strategies and infrastructures should be in place to ensure that the ROI Methodology is firmly integrated into programs. These elements may range from technology-based support processes to standardized guidelines, policies, and procedures. (Chapter Two covers policies in more detail.) In the integration stage, the ROI Methodology is universally and mutually understood by all stakeholders.

Some of the indicators that an organization or function is in the integration stage are the following:

- The organization or function has increased its focus on linking programs to the strategic directions of the organization.

- The organization or function displays a spirit of continuous improvement, innovation, and "out of the box" thinking about evaluation.

- The department or function is a key player in organizational change initiatives.

- The function's budget is growing.

- The function has strengthened collaborations with other key functional areas.

- The function is viewed as the internal expert on evaluation.

- The implementation team is able to routinely perform evaluation at best-of-class levels.

- Mentoring in evaluation practices is occurring, and there is management support for increased internal capabilities in evaluation.

- Best practices are identified and shared.

Several key tasks need attention at the integration stage.

1. Build and maintain stable links for integration of the change effort within other organizational systems through the following actions:

   - Build organizational self-reliance by reinforcing new behaviors and systems.
   - Position implementation of the ROI Methodology at the forefront of the unit's strategic plan.
   - Establish accountability everywhere, particularly away from senior leadership.
   - Enforce the consequences if desired performance levels are not being met.
   - Evaluate all environmental factors that are contributing to lack of progress.

2. Build and maintain cohesiveness and interdependence on all sides of the change effort by performing the following tasks:

   - Maintain strategic alliances with key stakeholder groups and individuals, and hold all stakeholders accountable for their commitments.
   - Emphasize the fact that comprehensive integration and implementation of the ROI Methodology may take several years; secure commitments for long-term support.
   - Plan informal rewards and recognition to support the achievement of milestones.
   - Keep in mind that many implementation team members must carry out their implementation assignments without relief from their daily job duties.

3. Ensure that the pace of organizational change does not compromise the integrity of the ROI Methodology by means of the following actions:

   - Challenge the implementation team to develop appropriate measures. Evaluate these measures continually to ensure that they are measuring desired change outcomes at appropriate intervals.

- Balance organizational priorities to protect the resources dedicated to implementation efforts. Examine the allocation of resources for implementation in order to discover any negative impacts on your organization's critical business issues.

- Recognize, analyze, and respond to all threats to the implementation of the ROI Methodology.

- Make the implementation team aware that senior management may not be close enough to the implementation to properly appraise its value to the organization and its level of accomplishment.

- Make compromises or adjustments in the implementation schedule as necessary to meet your organization's needs.

4. Share excitement about the ROI Methodology and its value to your organization through the following actions:

- Schedule and conduct periodic enthusiastic progress reviews, presented by the implementation team to senior management. These reviews should include the benefits of the process, including intangible benefits.

- Publicize success stories and best practices.

- Tailor statements of benefits to reinforce the business payoffs from the perspectives of multiple stakeholders.

Figure 4.2 illustrates key roles during each of the stages identified in this section. These stages of implementation do not necessarily occur in a linear fashion, one after another. However, the concerns and indicators of each stage are typical, to varying degrees, of most organizations as they begin to implement the ROI Methodology

Figure 4.2. Roles During Stages in Implementation of the ROI Methodology

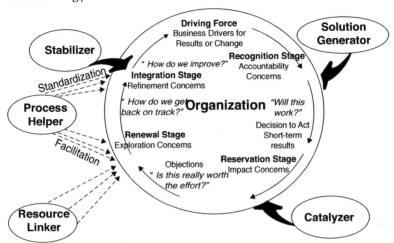

Source: Copyright © by Evaluation Works.

as standard practice. By understanding these stages, an evaluator or consultant can identify critical leverage points and assume roles that will accelerate organizational movement from one stage to the next. The key is to keep moving toward integration and avoid prolonged inertia.

Actions That Sustain the ROI Methodology

A few powerful actions that help sustain the ROI Methodology are covered in this section. They represent proven techniques for keeping the ROI Methodology vital for many years.

Publishing Case Studies

Targeted case studies foster internal capabilities in the ROI Methodology and build acceptance for its integration. Regular attention to selected impact studies is also important in order to show the following:

- Which programs have achieved success

- What organizational enablers or barriers occurred during the process of achieving desired results

- What new program expenditures are justified

Some organizations take the extra step of publishing case studies. Case studies can be published internally or externally. Internally, a printed case study becomes a useful document. It serves as a history of how the evaluation was conducted and serves as an excellent learning tool for others who wish to understand the methodology. In that situation, a case study can become the impetus for workshops for the staff.

Perhaps most important is the value that internally published case studies offer to prospective and current clients. It shows tangible evidence that an organizational function or program does make a difference. A case study in which the impact and the ROI are calculated may be one of the most effective ways of changing senior executives' perception of a function or department. A few larger organizations prepare case studies and publish them as a combined book. For example, SAP, Nokia, and the Department of Veterans Affairs published their own softcover casebooks, which served as excellent reference and learning tools and impressive documents to show others the influence and impact of their organizations.

Externally published case studies validate the success of an organizational function or unit. These studies are routinely published in books, journals, and the trade press. Having members of the staff write up and publish a case study provides recognition not only for the individual but for the unit and the organization as well. Sometimes, externally published case studies win awards from professional associations. For additional information on how case studies can be used, contact the ROI Institute, Inc., through its Web site at www.roiinstitute.net.

Holding Annual Progress Reviews

It is helpful to hold regular reviews for the senior executive team in order to show how well the ROI process is working. Such reviews are designed to show how the process is working, what success has been enjoyed, what is planned for the near future, and what is needed to keep it going. A typical agenda for an annual review includes the following topics:

- Review of previous year's programs

- Methods and levels of evaluation

- Results achieved from programs

- Significant deviations from expected results

- Basis for determining needs for the coming year

- Scheduled initiatives, programs, or services

- Proposed methods of evaluation

- Potential payoffs

- Problem areas or barriers to success

- Concerns from management (all levels)

These sessions should be framed as part of a continuous improvement process that will systematically do the following:

- Show the value derived from specific actions recommended in impact studies

- Track targeted improvements

- Track suggestions for continuous improvement

- Establish and review policy and practice in regard to mechanisms for communication

- Reinforce the role of management in building and sustaining a results-based culture

Calculating the ROI on Implementation of the ROI Methodology

Understanding the payoff from implementation of the ROI Methodology is important. No management team will support a process if they don't see its value. Individually, an impact study will show the value of a program; however, managers will quickly realize that conducting these studies requires significant resources. Does the entire process have a payoff? Some managers will ask for the ROI on implementation. The major positive impact associated with using the ROI Methodology over time includes the following:

- It can transform the role of a department or function within an organization.

- It increases alignment of programs with business needs.

- It improves the efficiency of solution design, development, and delivery by allowing program teams to

    Reduce costs

    Prevent a program from being implemented after the pilot process shows that it delivers no value

    Expand programs when other areas need the benefits of these programs

    Discontinue programs when they add no value

- It enhances the value of learning and development in an organization.

- It builds respect, support, and commitment from internal groups, including senior executives and major program sponsors.

Identifying potential payoffs early is important. Evaluating the preceding propositions to ensure that the evaluation process delivers on its promised value should be the role of the task force created during transition planning.

Reviewing Staff Roles

Program staff must continue to ensure that policies are implemented, that practices are followed, and that data are delivered in a timely manner. If the team members lose enthusiasm for implementation of the ROI Methodology or fail to complete each of the tasks, their actions will be perceived as a lack of commitment. Lack of commitment can be contagious and may cause others to lose support and commitment as well.

The importance of staff members' roles as advocates and champions who sustain the ROI Methodology over time can be illustrated by the experience of one health care organization. In this example, eleven employees involved in the original ROI Certification workshop, along with the senior executive team, were committed to adopting the ROI Methodology as a standard policy practice. However, members of the group described initial frustration with their own inexperience with the process and the difficulty of incorporating ROI programs into their already busy schedules. To deal with these challenges and continue moving forward, group members learned to find support in each other and in their shared beliefs about the value of the ROI Methodology to the business.

As the team continued to develop expertise in the ROI Methodology and began to successfully measure the results of programs, their confidence and enthusiasm galvanized partnerships with managers and the senior executive team, which in turn helped sustain the implementation throughout the organization.

To ensure continued organizational understanding, acceptance, and adoption of the methodology as routine, the team worked closely with senior executives across all functions to establish the ROI Methodology as a systemwide philosophy in which accountability for adding value was seen as the responsibility of everyone in the organization. In addition, the team assisted functional managers in conducting front-end needs assessments, provided learning opportunities on the ROI Methodology, and partnered with managers on subsequent ROI programs, with the goal of making all managers comfortable with the ROI Methodology. The program team catalyzed the successful implementation of the ROI Methodology throughout the organization.

In almost any situation, periodic reviews of staff roles and how they translate into day-to-day job descriptions will be helpful to ensure that

- Team members understand their responsibilities in making the process work as a systemwide approach

- Team members understand what they are supposed to accomplish and how and when they should do it

- Specific responsibilities are incorporated into job descriptions so that they become a routine part of work

This process can be integrated into midyear or annual performance appraisal processes or incorporated into individual developmental planning checkpoints and review dates. Any issues in managing evaluation outputs or work products associated with revised roles or the broader scope of the unit's results should also be a factor in annual budget planning.

Establishing Mechanisms for Continuous Improvement

Implementing the ROI Methodology and monitoring its progress within the realm of a single organizational function may be a relatively simple task. However, as the process becomes more visible and integrated within an organization, it becomes increasingly critical to build continuous improvement mechanisms into the process so that it remains credible and flexible over time. Some improvement mechanisms include the following:

- Progress reports that include recommendations from annual progress reviews

- Published success stories that document recommendations for improvement that were implemented

- Routine meetings in which lessons learned and solutions implemented are reviewed and tracked

Many organizations use a postmortem forum to review lessons learned from programs that involved considerable time or expense. Exhibit 4.1 provides an example of a lessons learned report that was used in a public sector organization. In this case, the report mirrored an organizational template and was used (a) as a supplement to impact study reports with programs that did not achieve desired results or (b) in lieu of an impact study report when the resources for an impact study were diverted and the impact study program was postponed or discontinued.

Finally, use the best practices described in the next section as a framework for continuous improvement.

Development of Best Practices

More than 3,000 organizations have taken the initiative to implement the ROI Methodology, based on the number of organizations that have participated in a comprehensive certification process designed to help individuals and teams implement the ROI

Exhibit 4.1. Lessons Learned Report

Version: Draft v0.2

Date:

Author:

Owner:

Table of Contents

About This Document

Related Documents

Summary of Changes

Reviews and Approvals

Distribution

Document Control Information

Chapter 1: Lessons Learned Report

1.1 Purpose of Document

1.2 Program Summary

    1.2.1 Program Background

    1.2.2 Program Milestones and Metrics

    1.2.3 Program Deliverables

1.3 Lessons Learned

    1.3.1 What Went Well

    1.3.2 What Didn't

    1.3.3 Enablers

    1.3.4 Barriers

    1.3.5 Suggestions for Improvement

1.4 Methodologies

    1.4.1 Program Management

    1.4.2 Resource Management

Exhibit 4.1. Lessons Learned Report (*Continued*)

1.4.3 System Design

1.4.4 Evaluation Management

1.5 Summary of Findings

1.6 Appendix: Tables, Figures, Exhibits

About This Document

Related Documents

This document should be used in conjunction with

Evaluation Policy and Procedures
Impact Study "X" Communication Plan
Impact Study "X" Data Collection Plan

Summary of Changes

This section records the history of changes to this document. Only the most significant changes are described here.

Version	Date	Author	Description of Change

When significant changes are made to this document, the version number will be increased by 1.0. When changes are made for clarity and reading ease only and no change is made to the meaning or intention of this document, the version number will be increased by 0.1.

(*Continued*)

Exhibit 4.1. Lessons Learned Report (*Continued*)

Reviews and Approvals

This document requires review and approval.

This document was approved by

Name	Role	Date

This document was reviewed by

Name	Role	Date

Distribution

This section lists all the persons or areas that will receive a copy of this document after it has been finalized.

Name	Area	Date

Document Control Information

At the end of this document is a labeled box indicating the end of text. _____

<Program Name> Lessons Learned Report
END OF DOCUMENT

Exhibit 4.1. Lessons Learned Report (*Continued*)

Chapter 1: Lessons Learned Report

1.1 Purpose of Document

Summarize the purpose of the Lessons Learned Report (that is, to pass on lessons learned that can be practically applied to other results-based evaluation programs).

1.2 Program Summary

1.2.1 Program Background

Summarize the business case for this results-based program and identify its key objectives in terms of needs/gaps in the following areas:

- Reaction to the program, including planned actions if appropriate

- Learning goals for program participants—desired knowledge and skills, as well as changes in perceptions

- Performance objectives—desired application and implementation of program learning

- Targeted business impact—metrics such as cost savings, productivity improvements, time reductions, increased sales, and so on

- As indicated, return on investment target—desired monetary benefits versus costs of the program

- Desired intangible benefits, such as employee satisfaction and customer satisfaction

Include summary information about the program sponsor, key stakeholders or client groups, and expected deliverables from the program.

(Continued)

Exhibit 4.1. Lessons Learned Report (*Continued*)

1.2.2 Program Milestones and Metrics

Summarize the relevant milestones and metrics of this program. These may include the following components in the chart below:

Program Components	Milestone or Metric
Estimated start date	
Estimated end date	
Actual start date	
Actual end date	
Schedule variance (days)	
Team size at start date	
Team size at end date	
Team size variance or attrition (individuals)	
Estimated program costs	
Actual program costs	
Cost variance (dollars)	
Estimated program monetary benefits	
Actual program monetary benefits	
Benefits variance (dollars)	
Program's return on investment	
Number of quality assurance reviews	
Number of incidents	

1.2.3 Program Deliverables

Deliverable	Due Date	Status/Comments

Exhibit 4.1. Lessons Learned Report (*Continued*)

1.3 Lessons Learned

Summarize what went well or did not and what can be improved as it applies to this results-based program.

1.3.1 *What Went Well*

1.3.2 *What Didn't*

1.3.3 *Enablers*

1.3.4 *Barriers*

1.3.5 *Suggestions for Improvement*

1.4 Methodologies

1.4.1 *Program Management*

Include recommendations for enhancement/modification to the program management methodology in this section. Include the following: program sponsorship; overall program planning; work plan; estimates; managing the work plan; managing resources; managing scope; managing communications, stakeholder expectations; managing quality; managing risk; and team characteristics.

Consider any recommendations related to the program management tools used during the program.

1.4.2 *Resource Management*

Include recommendations for enhancement/modification to the resource management (people, material, money) with regard to this program. Include how resources were approved, allocated, diverted, constrained, and/or used during the program life cycle. Also, include recommendations for improving resource use for future results-based programs.

(*Continued*)

Exhibit 4.1.Lessons Learned Report (*Continued*)

1.4.3 *System Design*

Include recommendations for enhancement/modification to the methodology used, including the assessment and design phase; the develop, build, and test phase; and the implementation and evaluation phase. Also include recommendations related to any tools used during the program.

1.4.4 *Evaluation Management*

Include recommendations for enhancement/modification to the evaluation management methodology used by the Workplace Learning function to achieve desired results. Include recommendations related to any of the following phases of evaluation management: evaluation planning, data collection, data analysis, and communication of results, including communication strengths/opportunities for improvement with key stakeholders. Include recommendations related to any data collection, survey, or testing tools or sampling groups used during the program.

1.5 Summary of Findings

Provide a high-level summary of your overall observation of this program, and state how these lessons can be used for continuous improvement and action planning with future results-based programs.

1.6 Appendix: Tables, Figures, Exhibits

Lessons Learned Report
END OF DOCUMENT

Methodology. Now that the ROI Methodology enjoys wide acceptance, the focus of many practitioners has turned to best practices for its implementation. The eleven best practices in this section represent the state of the art in organizations that have successfully implemented the ROI Methodology.

Best Practice 1

The ROI Methodology is implemented as a process improvement tool and not a performance evaluation tool. Staff acceptance is critical for successful implementation of the ROI Methodology. Few individuals or groups will want to use a tool that might ultimately be used to evaluate their performance. As a result, many organizations accept the notion of the ROI Methodology as a process improvement tool and communicate this posture early.

Best Practice 2

The ROI Methodology generates a micro-level scorecard with seven types of data. Each type of data reflects a distinct measure with a specific focus:

- *Level 0 (Inputs and Indicators)*: Measures the inputs into the program (people, resources, and so on)

- *Level 1 (Reaction and Planned Action)*: Measures participant satisfaction with the program and captures planned actions

- *Level 2 (Learning)*: Measures changes in knowledge, skills, and attitudes

- *Level 3 (Application)*: Measures changes in on-the-job behavior

- *Level 4 (Business Impact)*: Measures changes in business impact variables

- *Level 5 (ROI)*: Compares program benefits with program costs

- *Intangible Benefits*: Data that are purposely not converted to monetary values

The types of data shown in the preceding list constitute a scorecard of a program's performance, representing both qualitative and quantitative data, often taken at different time frames and from different sources.

Best Practice 3

ROI Methodology data collected at the program level are integrated to create a macro-level scorecard for an entire department or function. As more studies are conducted, their data are also incorporated. This concept was covered in more detail in Chapter One and illustrated in Figure 1.3. This approach requires that a few similar questions be asked each time data are gathered, so that consistent measures can be shown. Data from the responses are integrated, using technology, to create the macro-level scorecard.

Best Practice 4

ROI impact studies are conducted selectively, usually involving 5 to 10 percent of all programs and solutions. Programs that are usually targeted for Level 4 and 5 evaluations are those that are strategically focused, expensive, high-profile, controversial, or have management's interest. This does not mean that other programs are not evaluated. All programs should be evaluated at Level 1, the vast majority at Level 2, and many at Level 3, but only a few select programs are taken to Levels 4 and 5. More important, programs targeted for a Level 5 evaluation with an ROI calculation are, as best practice, evaluated at all five levels, up to and including ROI.

Best Practice 5

Setting ROI evaluation targets—the percentage of programs to be evaluated at each level—is another best practice. Considerations in developing target levels are the resources available and the feasibility of evaluation at each level. The target is usually 100 percent of programs at Level 1 and 5 to 10 percent of programs at Level 5.

Best Practice 6

Using a variety of data collection methods is a best practice in ROI analysis. Robust ROI evaluation is not restricted to a particular type of data collection method, such as monitoring business data. Instead, questionnaires, action plans, focus groups, and observations (among others) are used to develop the complete profile of seven types of data in the ROI Methodology.

Best Practice 7

For a specific ROI evaluation, the effects of programs and projects should be isolated from other factors. Although isolation of program effects is difficult, best-practice organizations realize that some method must be in place to show the direct contribution of a program to business impact. Many best-practice organizations use a variety of techniques, ranging from control group analysis to expert estimation, to address this issue in each evaluation. Some argue that this is too difficult. In reality, it must be done in order for executives to understand the relative contribution of a department or function. Otherwise, a temptation to slash the budgets of major programs may arise because executives see no clear connection between the programs and their business impact.

Best Practice 8

Business impact data are converted to monetary values. These days, simply reporting program outcomes—expressed in units of quality improvement, cycle-time reduction, turnover reduction, or percentage points of increased customer loyalty or job satisfaction—is not enough. The value in monetary terms is essential in calculating the ROI because an ROI calculation compares the benefits of a program with its costs. To allow this comparison, benefits must be valued in monetary terms, just as the costs are. Best-practice organizations use a full array of approaches to convert impact data to monetary values.

Best Practice 9

The ROI Methodology can be implemented for about 3 to 5 percent of a function's budget. One of the common fears about implementing the ROI Methodology is excessive cost in both time and funds. Best-practice organizations report that they can implement the ROI Methodology for roughly 3 to 5 percent of the total budget when they use evaluation targets as discussed in Best Practice 5.

When implementing the ROI Methodology, many organizations have migrated from a low level of investment (1 percent or less) to a higher level (3 to 5 percent) through a process of gradual budget increases. These increases sometimes come directly from the cost savings generated through the use of the ROI Methodology. In addition, cost-saving approaches can be used in resource-constrained environments.

Best Practice 10

Best practice organizations implement ROI forecasting routinely to improve the decision-making process. Senior executives sometimes ask for an ROI forecast before a program is launched. The credibility of the process is greatly increased by the use of conservative adjustments and built-in steps to secure input from the best experts. Forecasting is discussed in *Costs and ROI*, the fifth book in this series.

Best Practice 11

The ROI Methodology is used by best practice enterprises as a tool to strengthen and improve an organizational function or a department. A significant payoff for using the ROI Methodology over time is that it transforms the role of a function or department within an organization. Application of the process increases alignment with business needs; improves the efficiency of program design, development, and delivery; and increases the value of a function or department within an organization. Furthermore, it builds respect, support, and commitment from other internal groups, including senior executives and major program sponsors.

These best practices are evolving as hundreds of organizations use the ROI Methodology each year. Best practices underscore the progress that has been made in the methodology's implementation and use.

Summary

As in any change effort, constant attention and focus must be maintained in order to build and sustain the ROI Methodology over time. Without such attention, the methodology will ultimately fade out in an organization and be labeled as a passing fad. Paying regular attention to the ultimate business purposes of the evaluation process while maintaining its integrity is often one of the most challenging aspects of being an evaluation leader.

After the initial changes in measurement methods are implemented, the program team members may lose their sense of urgency and drift back to old cultures, mindsets, behaviors, and systems. Ultimately, the task of sustaining the ROI Methodology is not the sole responsibility of the implementation team; support must be generated from all stakeholders. A key challenge is securing and fostering ongoing support, cooperation, interaction, and dedication from all stakeholders in the evaluation process. Focusing on the following actions will help with these challenges.

- Remember that organizations migrate through predictable growth stages in the move from episodic implementation to long-term integration of the ROI Methodology.

- Look for specific indicators that implementation may be off track.

- Identify key roles and actions that will help your organization move successfully from one stage to the next.

- Continually renew and refresh commitment for the methodology across individual, process, and organizational levels so that it remains consistent, reliable, and credible in the eyes of stakeholders.

- Develop best practices for capturing organizational responses and lessons learned during the entire cycle of accountability.

- Continually seek best-practice examples from professional associations, training literature, journals, case studies, colleagues, and the ROI Network.

Exhibit 4.2 presents a checklist that can help leaders sustain momentum for implementation of the ROI Methodology within an organization.

Now that the typical stages of ROI Methodology implementation have been identified, roles in the implementation process have been defined, and specific enabling strategies to assist in this effort have been outlined, it's time to commit to action. Exhibit 4.3 will help you plan your action steps.

Exhibit 4.2. Checklist for Implementation of the ROI Methodology

Enabling Strategies	Yes	No
Have stages of ROI implementation been identified?	☐	☐
Have roles been assigned to facilitate organizational movement toward the integration stage?	☐	☐
Are case studies developed on a regular basis?	☐	☐
Has the ROI on the ROI Methodology been effectively and routinely communicated to stakeholders?	☐	☐
Are staff roles in implementation of the ROI Methodology regularly reviewed, revised, and updated?	☐	☐
Are continuous improvement mechanisms in place for the ROI Methodology?	☐	☐
Are lessons learned captured and reported?	☐	☐
Are best practices routinely identified?	☐	☐
Are best practices routinely applied?	☐	☐
Are best practices routinely shared?	☐	☐

Final Thoughts

This chapter focuses on the actions needed to build and sustain the ROI Methodology over time. Emphasizing the ROI Methodology as a long-term process improvement tool adds value and keeps it from becoming a passing fad or short-term phenomenon. If ROI evaluation is not an integral part of the way a functional unit does business, then the accountability for programs and projects will ultimately suffer. Specifically, this chapter helps to

- Identify organizational stages of ROI Methodology implementation

- Define roles in facilitating movement from one stage to the next

Exhibit 4.3 Action Planning for Enabling Strategies

1. Commit to take action on one or more of the following enabling strategies defined in this chapter:

   a. Implement specific impact or case studies.

   b. Schedule and enthusiastically conduct periodic review sessions.

   c. Calculate the payoff of the ROI Methodology in order to show that it is worthwhile.

   d. Build continuous improvement mechanisms to ensure that enhancements to the process are routinely explored.

   e. Routinely review roles.

   f. Publicize success stories and identify best practices.

2. Identify one enabling strategy or continuous improvement action on which you are willing to focus for the next thirty days. It can be an action that you will continue to do or an action to attempt in the future. Write down this strategy or continuous improvement action and the date by which you will act:

   _____

   _____

3. Identify a person with whom you will share your plan, and select a date when you both will review your progress (for example, thirty days from initiation).
   Action plan partner: _____
   Review date: _____

- Identify inhibitors and enablers to successful implementation of the ROI Methodology

- Apply enabling strategies and specific actions to sustain the implementation of the ROI Methodology over time

All the tips and tools in this book will support implementation of the ROI Methodology as a mainstream, value-added activity.

Reference

Scott, C., and Jaffe, D. *Getting Your Organization to Change*. Menlo Park, CA.: Crisp, 1999.

Index

About the Authors

Jack J. Phillips, Ph.D., a world-renowned expert on accountability, measurement, and evaluation, provides consulting services for Fortune 500 companies and major global organizations. The author or editor of more than fifty books, Phillips conducts workshops and makes conference presentations throughout the world.

His expertise in measurement and evaluation is based on more than twenty-seven years of corporate experience in the aerospace, textile, metals, construction materials, and banking industries. Phillips has served as training and development manager at two Fortune 500 firms, as senior human resources officer at two firms, as president of a regional bank, and as management professor at a major state university. This background led Phillips to develop the ROI Methodology, a revolutionary process that provides bottom-line figures and accountability for all types of learning, performance improvement, human resources, technology, and public policy programs.

Phillips regularly consults with clients in manufacturing, service, and government organizations in forty-four countries in North and South America, Europe, Africa, Australia, and Asia.

Books most recently authored by Phillips include *Show Me the Money: How to Determine ROI in People, Projects, and Programs* (Berrett-Koehler, 2007); *The Value of Learning* (Pfeiffer, 2007); *How to Build a Successful Consulting Practice* (McGraw-Hill, 2006);

Investing in Your Company's Human Capital: Strategies to Avoid Spending Too Much or Too Little (Amacom, 2005); *Proving the Value of HR: How and Why to Measure ROI* (Society for Human Resource Management, 2005); *The Leadership Scorecard* (Butterworth-Heinemann, 2004); *Managing Employee Retention* (Butterworth-Heinemann, 2003); *Return on Investment in Training and Performance Improvement Programs*, 2nd edition (Butterworth-Heinemann, 2003); *The Project Management Scorecard* (Butterworth-Heinemann, 2002); *How to Measure Training Results* (McGraw-Hill, 2002); *The Human Resources Scorecard: Measuring the Return on Investment* (Butterworth-Heinemann, 2001); *The Consultant's Scorecard* (McGraw-Hill, 2000); and *Performance Analysis and Consulting* (ASTD, 2000). Phillips served as series editor for the In Action casebook series of the American Society for Training and Development (ASTD), an ambitious publishing project featuring thirty titles. He currently serves as series editor for Butterworth-Heinemann's Improving Human Performance series and for Pfeiffer's new Measurement and Evaluation series.

Phillips has received several awards for his books and his work. The Society for Human Resource Management presented him with an award for one of his books and honored a Phillips ROI study with its highest award for creativity. ASTD gave him its highest award, Distinguished Contribution to Workplace Learning and Development. *Meeting News* named Phillips one of the twenty-five most influential people in the meetings and events industry, based on his work on ROI within the industry.

Phillips holds undergraduate degrees in electrical engineering, physics, and mathematics; a master's degree in decision sciences from Georgia State University; and a Ph.D. degree in human resources management from the University of Alabama.

Jack Phillips has served on the boards of several private businesses—including two NASDAQ companies—and several associations, including ASTD, and nonprofit organizations. He is chairman of the ROI Institute, Inc., and can be reached at (205) 678-8101, or by e-mail at jack@roiinstitute.net.

Wendi Friedman Tush, M.B.A., is president of the Lexicomm Group, a strategic communications consulting company. The Lexicomm Group specializes in "thought leadership" marketing. The company raises executive profiles, revitalizes corporate identities, changes hearts and minds, and provides crisis management for companies and their key executives.

Tush has rebranded, repositioned, and created strategic communications and public relations campaigns for many CEOs and companies, including DuPont, Samsung, Malcolm Bricklin and Visionary Vehicles, David Silverstein and Breakthrough Management Group, Jeff Johnson and Cano Petroleum, Cybersettle, Anvil Knitwear, Gottaplay, iDNA, and US Luggage.

Prior to her career in communications consulting, Tush was a broadcast journalist for CNN, FNN, CNBC, and VH1. She holds a bachelor of arts degree in psychology from Cornell University and a master's degree in business administration from Columbia University.

Pfeiffer Publications Guide

This guide is designed to familiarize you with the various types of Pfeiffer publications. The formats section describes the various types of products that we publish; the methodologies section describes the many different ways that content might be provided within a product. We also provide a list of the topic areas in which we publish.

FORMATS

In addition to its extensive book-publishing program, Pfeiffer offers content in an array of formats, from fieldbooks for the practitioner to complete, ready-to-use training packages that support group learning.

FIELDBOOK Designed to provide information and guidance to practitioners in the midst of action. Most fieldbooks are companions to another, sometimes earlier, work, from which its ideas are derived; the fieldbook makes practical what was theoretical in the original text. Fieldbooks can certainly be read from cover to cover. More likely, though, you'll find yourself bouncing around following a particular theme, or dipping in as the mood, and the situation, dictate.

HANDBOOK A contributed volume of work on a single topic, comprising an eclectic mix of ideas, case studies, and best practices sourced by practitioners and experts in the field.

An editor or team of editors usually is appointed to seek out contributors and to evaluate content for relevance to the topic. Think of a handbook not as a ready-to-eat meal, but as a cookbook of ingredients that enables you to create the most fitting experience for the occasion.

RESOURCE Materials designed to support group learning. They come in many forms: a complete, ready-to-use exercise (such as a game); a comprehensive resource on one topic (such as conflict management) containing a variety of methods and approaches; or a collection of like-minded activities (such as icebreakers) on multiple subjects and situations.

TRAINING PACKAGE An entire, ready-to-use learning program that focuses on a particular topic or skill. All packages comprise a guide for the facilitator/trainer and a workbook for the participants. Some packages are supported with additional media—such as video—or learning aids, instruments, or other devices to help participants understand concepts or practice and develop skills.

- *Facilitator/trainer's guide* Contains an introduction to the program, advice on how to organize and facilitate the learning event, and step-by-step instructor notes. The guide also contains copies of presentation materials—handouts, presentations, and overhead designs, for example—used in the program.

- *Participant's workbook* Contains exercises and reading materials that support the learning goal and serves as a valuable reference and support guide for participants in the weeks and months that follow the learning event. Typically, each participant will require his or her own workbook.

ELECTRONIC CD-ROMs and web-based products transform static Pfeiffer content into dynamic, interactive experiences. Designed to take advantage of the searchability, automation, and ease-of-use that technology provides, our e-products bring convenience and immediate accessibility to your workspace.

METHODOLOGIES

CASE STUDY A presentation, in narrative form, of an actual event that has occurred inside an organization. Case studies are not prescriptive, nor are they used to prove a point; they are designed to develop critical analysis and decision-making skills. A case study has a specific time frame, specifies a sequence of events, is narrative in structure, and contains a plot structure—an issue (what should be/have been done?). Use case studies when the goal is to enable participants to apply previously learned theories to the circumstances in the case, decide what is pertinent, identify the real issues, decide what should have been done, and develop a plan of action.

ENERGIZER A short activity that develops readiness for the next session or learning event. Energizers are most commonly used after a break or lunch to stimulate or refocus the group. Many involve some form of physical activity, so they are a useful way to counter post-lunch lethargy. Other uses include transitioning from one topic to another, where "mental" distancing is important.

EXPERIENTIAL LEARNING ACTIVITY (ELA) A facilitator-led intervention that moves participants through the learning cycle from experience to application (also known as a Structured Experience). ELAs are carefully thought-out designs in which there is a definite learning purpose and intended outcome. Each step—everything that participants do during the activity—facilitates the accomplishment of the stated goal. Each ELA includes complete instructions for facilitating the intervention and a clear statement of goals, suggested group size and timing, materials required, an explanation of the process, and, where appropriate, possible variations to the activity. (For more detail on Experiential Learning Activities, see the Introduction to the *Reference Guide to Handbooks and Annuals*, 1999 edition, Pfeiffer, San Francisco.)

GAME A group activity that has the purpose of fostering team spirit and togetherness in addition to the achievement of a pre-stated goal. Usually contrived—undertaking a desert expedition, for example—this type of learning method offers an engaging means for participants to demonstrate and practice business and interpersonal skills. Games are effective for team building and personal development mainly because the goal is subordinate to the process—the means through which participants reach decisions, collaborate, communicate, and generate trust and understanding. Games often engage teams in "friendly" competition.

ICEBREAKER A (usually) short activity designed to help participants overcome initial anxiety in a training session and/or to acquaint the participants with one another. An icebreaker can be a fun activity or can be tied to specific topics or training goals. While a useful tool in itself, the icebreaker comes into its own in situations where tension or resistance exists within a group.

INSTRUMENT A device used to assess, appraise, evaluate, describe, classify, and summarize various aspects of human behavior. The term used to describe an instrument depends primarily on its format and purpose. These terms include survey, questionnaire, inventory, diagnostic, survey, and poll. Some uses of instruments include providing instrumental feedback to group members, studying here-and-now processes or functioning within a group, manipulating group composition, and evaluating outcomes of training and other interventions.

Instruments are popular in the training and HR field because, in general, more growth can occur if an individual is provided with a method for focusing specifically on his or her own behavior. Instruments also are used to obtain information that will serve as a basis for change and to assist in workforce planning efforts.

Paper-and-pencil tests still dominate the instrument landscape with a typical package comprising a facilitator's guide, which offers advice on administering the instrument and interpreting the collected data, and an initial set of instruments. Additional instruments are available separately. Pfeiffer, though, is investing heavily in e-instruments. Electronic instrumentation provides effortless distribution and, for larger groups particularly, offers advantages over paper-and-pencil tests in the time it takes to analyze data and provide feedback.

LECTURETTE A short talk that provides an explanation of a principle, model, or process that is pertinent to the participants' current learning needs. A lecturette is intended to establish a common language bond between the trainer and the participants by providing a mutual frame of reference. Use a lecturette as an introduction to a group activity or event, as an interjection during an event, or as a handout.

MODEL A graphic depiction of a system or process and the relationship among its elements. Models provide a frame of reference and something more tangible, and more easily remembered, than a verbal explanation. They also give participants something to "go on," enabling them to track their own progress as they experience the dynamics, processes, and relationships being depicted in the model.

ROLE PLAY A technique in which people assume a role in a situation/scenario: a customer service rep in an angry-customer exchange, for example. The way in which the role is approached is then discussed and feedback is offered. The role play is often repeated using a different approach and/or incorporating changes made based on feedback received. In other words, role playing is a spontaneous interaction involving realistic behavior under artificial (and safe) conditions.

SIMULATION A methodology for understanding the interrelationships among components of a system or process. Simulations differ from games in that they test or use a model that depicts or mirrors some aspect of reality in form, if not necessarily in content. Learning occurs by studying the effects of change on one or more factors of the model. Simulations are commonly used to test hypotheses about what happens in a system—often referred to as "what if?" analysis—or to examine best-case/worst-case scenarios.

THEORY A presentation of an idea from a conjectural perspective. Theories are useful because they encourage us to examine behavior and phenomena through a different lens.

TOPICS

The twin goals of providing effective and practical solutions for workforce training and organization development and meeting the educational needs of training and human resource professionals shape Pfeiffer's publishing program. Core topics include the following:

Leadership & Management

Communication & Presentation

Coaching & Mentoring

Training & Development

E-Learning

Teams & Collaboration

OD & Strategic Planning

Human Resources

Consulting

What will you find on pfeiffer.com?

• The best in workplace performance solutions for training and HR professionals

• Downloadable training tools, exercises, and content

• Web-exclusive offers

• Training tips, articles, and news

• Seamless on-line ordering

• Author guidelines, information on becoming a Pfeiffer Affiliate, and much more

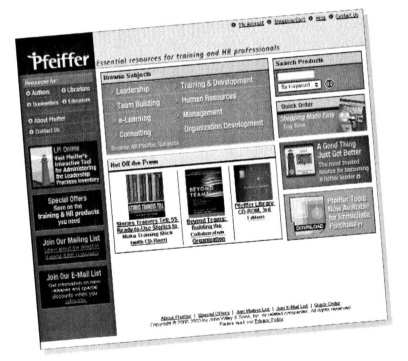

Discover more at www.pfeiffer.com

Measurement and Evaluation Series

Series Editors
Patricia Pulliam Phillips, Ph.D., and Jack J. Phillips, Ph.D.

A six-book set that provides a step-by-step system for planning, measuring, calculating, and communicating evaluation and Return-on-Investment for training and development, featuring:

- Detailed templates
- Complete plans
- Ready-to-use tools
- Real-world case examples

The M&E Series features:

1. *ROI Fundamentals: Why and When to Measure ROI*
   (978-0-7879-8716-9)

2. *Data Collection: Planning For and Collecting All Types of Data*
   (978-0-7879-8718-3)

3. *Isolation of Results: Defining the Impact of the Program*
   (978-0-7879-8719-0)

4. *Data Conversion: Calculating the Monetary Benefits*
   (978-0-7879-8720-6)

5. *Costs and ROI: Evaluating at the Ultimate Level*
   (978-0-7879-8721-3)

6. *Communication and Implementation: Sustaining the Practice*
   (978-0-7879-8722-0)

Plus, the *ROI in Action Casebook* (978-0-7879-8717-6) covers all the major workplace learning and performance applications, including Leadership Development, Sales Training, Performance Improvement, Technical Skills Training, Information Technology Training, Orientation and OJT, and Supervisor Training.

The **ROI Methodology** is a comprehensive measurement and evaluation process that collects six types of measures: Reaction, Satisfaction, and Planned Action; Learning; Application and Implementation; Business Impact; Return on Investment; and Intangible Measures. The process provides a step-by-step system for evaluation and planning, data collection, data analysis, and reporting. It is appropriate for the measurement and evaluation of *all* kinds of performance improvement programs and activities, including training and development, learning, human resources, coaching, meetings and events, consulting, and project management.

Special Offer from the ROI Institute

Send for your own ROI Process Model, an indispensable tool for implementing and presenting ROI in your organization. The ROI Institute is offering an exclusive gift to readers of The Measurement and Evaluation Series. This 11" x 25" multicolor foldout shows the ROI Methodology flow model and the key issues surrounding the implementation of the ROI Methodology. This easy-to-understand overview of the ROI Methodology has proven invaluable to countless professionals when implementing the ROI Methodology. Please return this page or e-mail your information to the address below to receive your free foldout (a $6.00 value). Please check your area(s) of interest in ROI.

Please send me the ROI Process Model described in the book. I am interested in learning more about the following ROI materials and services:

☐ Workshops and briefing on ROI   ☐ ROI consulting services
☐ Books and support materials on ROI   ☐ ROI Network information
☐ Certification in the ROI Methodology   ☐ ROI benchmarking
☐ ROI software   ☐ ROI research

Name _____

Title _____

Organization _____

Address _____

Phone _____

E-mail Address _____

Functional area of interest:

☐ Learning and Development/Performance Improvement
☐ Human Resources/Human Capital
☐ Public Relations/Community Affairs/Government Relations
☐ Consulting
☐ Sales/Marketing
☐ Technology/IT Systems
☐ Project Management Solutions
☐ Quality/Six Sigma
☐ Operations/Methods/Engineering
☐ Research and Development/Innovations
☐ Finance/Compliance
☐ Logistics/Distribution/Supply Chain
☐ Public Policy Initiatives
☐ Social Programs
☐ Other (Please Specify) _____

Organizational Level

☐ executive   ☐ management   ☐ consultant   ☐ specialist
☐ student   ☐ evaluator   ☐ researcher

Return this form or contact   The ROI Institute
                                    P.O. Box 380637
                                    Birmingham, AL 35238-0637

Or e-mail information to info@roiinstitute.net
Please allow four to six weeks for delivery.